GOATGAL'S DATING MANUAL

Barnyard Wisdom:
The Secret to Attracting Love

by
Peggy Kligman

Pandoshus Press

GOATGAL'S DATING MANUAL
Barnyard Wisdom: The Secret to Attracting Love
by
Peggy Kligman

Copyright © Peggy Kligman, 2012
ISBN-13: 978-0615718842

Pandoshus Press
El Paso, TX 79912

Dedication

To my parents, Sid and Fay. If not for your devotion to one an-other—for more than sixty years—I would have thought love was for the birds. You showed me otherwise.

Contents

Contents

Acknowledgments

I thank all my exes for joining me on love's quest. Some of you I have lost touch with but, of course, I wish you well. Those others from my past that remain in my life, I thank you for your unconditional friendship beyond the relationship we once had. With each one, I've been taught many lessons, all of which steer me back to my own heart and the desires it holds.

I thank my parents who exemplify love and devotion. When asked what the secret is to a long and lasting marriage, Mother is quick to reply, *"Never go to bed angry."* (This wisdom works especially well in the golden years when short-term memory is often a blur.) Along with my parents love, I thank my daughter and her devoted husband for surrounding me with their love and the love of grandkids.

To my happily married and happily single friends: Margie and Ray Reich, Ginny Fischer, Elaine Corn, Dotty Griffith, David Soohoo, Pam Stringer, Michael Wehrli, Renee Arnold, Christine Zolper, Linda Catoggio, Barbara Antebi, Paula Yardeni, Mary Murray-Jenkins, Ruth and Steve McGrew, Stan and Margie Ball, Louann Feuerstein, Lynn Provenzano, Katie Lopez and Carlos Hernandez. Thank you for our long conversations about love and dating. The same goes for those participants who timidly ventured into my singles Goat Game events and soon relaxed into the revelry of swapping good and *baahd* dating experiences.

To the friendships formed in the mental health field, thank you for your endorsements of the Goat Game. A special thanks to psychotherapist Kimberly Brenner for participating as a "Goat Game Therapist" at many of my events and for being my sounding board and a cherished friend.

To my editor Lucia Zimmitti, thank you for your

guidance throughout this book's project. Your expertise in the field of editing *and* a successful marriage assured me that the *GoatGal's Dating MANual* was in capable and loving hands.

To my graphic artist and website developer, Guillermo Delgado, for your creativity in developing the branded illustrations of the book cover, logo, and game along with the website.

To the original artist of the Goat Game, Francisco Romero and graphic illustrator Geronimo Garcia, a special thanks for planting those creative seeds.

Heartfelt thanks to the young girl, Carolina Zamorano, who along with her parents invited me over to play with the goats at her goat farm. There's nothing like a crisp autumn morning frolicking in the goat pens! It was great fun.

I thank *all* the poets, songwriters, artists, movie script writers, and romantic novelists who offer-up the hope of love when, at times, it seems so distant.

I thank the courteous gentlemen who open those doors for us, offer us roses and listen to our hearts.

Above all, I thank you single ladies who haven't given up on love and are willing to give it another chance.

Disclaimer

This *MANual* and the *Goat Game* is for personal entertainment purposes only. It is a light-hearted approach of examining one's dating behaviors and should not be considered legal, professional, or personal advice. Although it is utilized by some mental health professionals, it is not to be misconstrued as a substitute for therapy. Author and game creator Peggy Kligman is not a mental health professional and makes no claim as such. She assumes no responsibility for errors, accuracy, omissions or any other interpretations of this subject matter.

If while working through this *MANual* you find it difficult to release the memories of a traumatic past and feel unable to move forward toward a loving relationship, consult a licensed therapist to determine the best course of action for you.

The names used throughout the *MANual* have been changed to protect the privacy of individuals who have shared their experiences. These stories are used as a means of illustrating a point. These illustrations do not necessarily conform 100% to actual occurrences.

Goat Game is a registered trademark assigned to Pandoshus, LLC, and is protected as the property ascribed to Peggy Kligman, creator of the game. *GoatGal's Dating MANual* is copyrighted with all rights reserved. It is illegal to copy or distribute any part of this work without written permission from author Peggy Kligman or Pandoshus, LLC.

Preface

"Using the Goat Game is a great way to see how we sabotage relationships. Gaming makes it fun and not confronting. When we can laugh at ourselves, we learn and change."

~Kimberly Brenner, LCSW

As the creator of the Goat Game, it's not unusual to elicit curiosity about what it is I do. I overheard two men, within earshot, talking about my game. One said to the other, "It must be for women who enjoy making hay out of male-bashing." It was then that I remembered goats have a *baahd* rap. It is true that men who exhibit crude behaviors are often labeled lecherous old goats. For that matter, the same can be said for women.

When I set out to create the game, my intent was not to denigrate the male by comparing him to the goat persona as though it were a despicable attribute. Quite the contrary, I have a fondness for goats *and* men.

My interest in goats began years ago, after discovering a goat farm near my home. This was back in the days when I felt stuck in an unloving marriage. While spying on these hoofed beasts as a distraction from my woes, I witnessed their spontaneous playful nature. Secretly I yearned for joy, but under the weight of my troubles it was unobtainable.

In those days, I wondered why love had forsaken me. Thank goodness I witnessed love exhibited by the tender devotion between my parents and other lucky in-love couples. If not, I might have grown bitter, believing love was a pie-in-the-sky illusion supplied by the film industry to boost chick flick ticket sales. Years later, I divorced and moved away from the goat farm, but ending the marriage didn't end my suffering. I continued to attract unloving relationships. Down on my dating luck, I concluded the problem wasn't *out there*, it was *in here*, inside of me.

Opting to take a break from relationships, I spent my time delving inward searching how and why these cycles began. Intuitively I believed that once its source was revealed, I could find a way to let go of my misery and break from those patterns. My hope was to shed the anger and bitterness of my past as a means to lift my spirits with hope for love in my future.

Such a solitary task was arduous, and I needed help. It came in the form of the goat as my muse. I journaled and sketched my doomed romances through the non-threatening persona of these barnyard animals, depicting myself as a goat-gal and those whom I attracted (the good and the *baahd*) as the goat. I looked back on those hasty *roll in the hay* encounters (Step 9) and irresponsible *scapegoating* (blaming others for my misery), but in a less shameful way via a game format. Through the mischievous dating shenanigans of these rambunctious frolicking goodtime characters, the Goat Game was born, teaching me the lessons of my past.

"The goat becomes the professor whenever teachers can't be found."
~ Turkish proverb

In 2003, the first edition of the game was developed. With endorsements from mental health professionals, its *barnyard wisdom* took hold as a psychotherapy tool. Taking it a step further, I introduced the game to singles by facilitating dating workshops at coffee shops, patio bars and private parties. This women's game appeals to not only females, but males, too. By inviting both sexes to join in, it serves as an interactive ice-breaker.

Eight years later, the card deck edition came along as a condensed version of the original board game. It's played a bit differently but lends itself as an ice-breaker similar to its predecessor. More importantly, this deck goes hand-in-hand with the teachings of the *MANual*. While working through the following Steps, you'll find the game cards sampled throughout. *Loving Relationship Cards* trump *Roll in the Hay Cards* and *Flirt Cards* offer valuable dating tips.

The *GoatGal's Dating MANual* and its game is a playful illustration of goatish behaviors and their likeness to good and *baahd* human behaviors while unraveling the mystery of dating in a light-hearted way.

After completing the journal exercises in this *MANual*, play the game and test your knowledge of *barnyard wisdom*. Throw a Goat Game party, invite your friends over and have some fun! Or start your own Goat Game group by becoming a facilitator in your community. Goat Game products are available for purchase through the website at goatgame.com.

"Play energizes us and enlivens us. It eases our burdens. It renews our natural sense of optimism and opens us up to new possibilities." ~
Stuart Brown, MD

Is Barnyard Wisdom for You?

B-A-R-N-Y-A-R-D: **By-Accepting-Responsibility-Now-Your-**
Actions-Reflect-your-Destiny

We've been told good fortune shines on those hard working individuals who hold themselves accountable. If so, then why do many of us who follow such common sense guidelines fail at love? To answer this million-dollar question requires one to admit *what* went wrong in order to find out *why* it did. Yet looking back on one's track record of relationship failures is horrid. And to have to confess one chose unwisely or was irresponsible and, even worse, reckless for breaking others' hearts (including one's own) is an even more horrid request. It's easier to shrug it off as *unlucky in love*. That is, until we make a decision to truly listen to our heart's desire. To do so we must remove the bubble wrap we placed around it.

As I went to task unraveling the protective coating of my heart, I found saved memories, some I held dear and some not so dear. The not so dear ones were those unfulfilled expectations and heartbreaks that overshadowed my heart's desire. It's no wonder I couldn't connect to another's heart when I was detached from my own.

Barnyard wisdom is how I broke down those blockades by shedding light on my dating behaviors, thus, restoring brokenheartedness to wholeheartedness. The pay-off of doing the personal growth work was evident. I ended the cycles of dating dysfunction and was set free to attract healthy and loving relationships. The same can happen to you!

On the following page, take the *Barnyard Wisdom Quiz*. If you answer "yes" to any of these questions, recite the *GoatGal's Pledge* to get you started on changing your dating luck!

Barnyard Wisdom Quiz

- Are you clueless when it comes to dating?

- Do you find yourself in and out of relationships that bring out the worst in you?

- Do you want out of your current relationship but don't know how to let go?

- Have you lost trust in the notion of true love?

- Do you hate being single so much that you'll settle for just any relationship?

- Do you more often choose incompatible mates and, therefore feel unloved in your relationships?

- Do you attract the same types of goats and wonder why it never works out?

- Do you believe love's quest is too heart-wrenching and not worth the pain?

- Do you cast blame, making your ex out to be the *baahd* goat (scapegoating)?

- Do you use sex as a ploy to capture love and later wonder why it doesn't last?

Barnyard Wisdom Definitions

Goat:
A potential mate.

Scapegoating:
Blaming others for one's misery.

Goatish Behavior:
Conniving, manipulative, and controlling behavior unbecoming to a lady or gentleman.

Roll in the Hay:
Engaging in sex before establishing a loving and trusting relationship. Seemingly consensual but more often an impulsive sexual gratification used as a manipulation (a pretense for love or other objective). Often called a romp, fling, affair, and a *slam-bam-thank-you-ma'am*.

Loving Relationship:
Sincere and trusting with deeply felt emotional affection and caring for one another's well being.

Flirt:
Showing attraction and a romantic interest towards another. Can be subtle and coquettish and at other times transparent and obvious.

Tease:
Seemingly seductive with sexual overtures as a ploy for something other than sex.

How to Use this *MANual*

Think of yourself as the goatgal on love's quest for your goat. (Or, whatever is your sexual preference.) Throughout the *MANual*, I've used she/he pronouns to delineate the concept of you as the "she" and your mate as the "he.")

Barnyard wisdom is mapped out in a specific order to transition you from dating failures into dating success in a wholehearted way. There are no shortcuts for getting you relationship ready. That said, it's not advisable to dive head first into Step 8's *Flirting Finesse* before completing the previous Steps in preparing your heart. After completing all the Steps (no skipping around), *then* you are equipped to handle those situations that inevitably reveal themselves while out there on love's quest. Expect some set-backs along the way which might bring you back a Step or two.

Each Step is followed up with a QnR (Questions on Reflection) with a card from the game deck guiding you inward to assist you in highlighting those issues and behaviors circumventing your relationship success. Read them over with care. Notice the emotions that surface. These feelings are attached to memories from your past. Write out (journal through) those findings. This is not a manuscript needing spell-check or correct punctuation. It's your inner thoughts only. Let it flow out of you and onto the paper.

Journaling reveals where your issues originated. Once identified, the fix can be made eradicating those self-defeating patterns by replacing them with healthier behavioral skills to better attract a suitable mate.

"Journal writing is a voyage to the interior."

~ Christina Baldwin

GoatGal's Pledge

*I accept responsibility for relationships I
attract and for the behaviors I exhibit.
I cease placing blame on others. Instead,
I diligently examine my expectations,
motives, manipulations and conduct.
And by learning the lessons from my past,
I release old patterns of dysfunction while
rebuilding love and trust within, thereby
initiating healthier relationship skills.*

GOATGAL'S
DATING MANUAL

Step 1: Relationship Failures
Lesson Learned Rebuilds Trust in YOU!

♨ **Coffee was first discovered when goat herders noticed their goats behaving energetically (more so than usual) after nibbling on coffee beans.**

You and your friends talk about it, dream about it, and watch movies about it. You know "it" happens to others, so why not you? You wonder if by chance *it* could be better understood, and thus, made more recognizable and attainable as discussed and questioned about in a romantic comedy movie, *French Film*. Midway into the story, the leading male queries his therapist, *"How do you know when it's love?"*

To paraphrase the scripted lines as best as I remember, his male therapist answers in a sexy deep French accent: *"Love is everything! You're in love when suddenly everything changes. You're sipping on coffee and its taste is more delicious. You notice how her fingers caress the cup. You gaze deep into her eyes. Like diving into a pool, you are swimming in her soul. That's how you know."*

In the final scene (of this or some other similar romance movie) and after the leading male is done messing around with someone else, he looks into her eyes with that *love-is-everything* expression. And in that moment he is struck with: *She's the one!* The orchestra delivers a final crescendo. The camera spins, encircling the in-love couple. The credits roll.

You gobble up the last kernel of buttered popcorn and mutter, *Why can't this happen to me?* So you search and search for a *love-is-everything* connection. You romp through the pastures nibbling on this and that. More often than not, such high-spirited frivolity lands you in goat pens far, far away from your heart's desire. Weary and embittered, you lose faith, believing love isn't all it's cracked up to be while your heart takes a beating at every turn.

If you are like I was, a thrill seeker attracting those types of *baahd* sexy goats even though they ended up betraying you, look inward for the real reason. Upon close examination, this doomsday attraction could stem from trust issues manifesting itself as a magnet for betrayals. Unaddressed, trust issues from long ago can play their dirty hand forever — same scenarios but with different players.

The following passage, as spoken by Charlotte Bronte's Jane Eyre, illustrates the significance of recovering one's self-trust as crucial to one's capacities for moving away from dysfunction.

> *"I still felt as a wanderer on the face of the earth; but I experienced firmer trust in myself and my own powers, and less withering dread of oppression. The gaping wound of my wrongs, too, was now quite healed; and the flame of resentment extinguished."*

Whether or not you have trust issues, navigating through today's fast-paced singles scene can mess with one's self-respect and confidence. One moment you think love has found you, and the next moment he's flirting with another's profile pix on a social network site.

Before you turn your heart inside out *blocking* and *unfriending* those you suspect might be to blame, find your meaning of trust. Trust issues are easily resolved once insecurities are revealed. Such discoveries will gain you insight in how to first trust and love YOU in the way you expect others to do. It's more about building trust within (by fulfilling one's own needs) so you can identify it (or the lack thereof) in others.

In the following QnR, begin with your last relationship and work backwards. (As author Pearl Buck said, *"If you want to understand today, you have to search yesterday.")* Continue journaling until you get to the original source of pain festering throughout your subsequent relationships. It may go all the way back to the first time your heart was broken or to family issues from an unhealed hurt where trust was lost.

The first three Steps of this *MANual* you are asked to review your past. If you haven't suffered through patterns of broken-hearted romances or unresolved trust issues, still review these Steps just in case you inadvertently stumble on a not so loving relationship while on love's quest. With every misstep is a lesson learned.

Hang on, dear reader. If suddenly you're overwhelmed with dread about delving inward and more anxious to get to the part about releasing your aphrodisiac, don't fret. Your special someone waits patiently for *you* to discover loveable YOU!

"Your task is not to seek for love, but merely to seek and find all the barriers within yourself that you have built against it."
~ Rumi

Key Points
Rules 4 Reviewing Your Past

✪ **Examine the past.** To initiate change, one must be willing to look back in order to regain hope for the future. Eliminating what doesn't work helps you illuminate what does.

✪ **Chart the patterns of behaviors.** Whatever is playing over and over in your failed relationships points you toward issues in need of resolution and healing.

✪ **Identify your expectations.** Such neediness has been the magnet attracting unsuitable mates and unhealthy relationships.

✪ **Rebuild trust and love within.** Fulfill your needs so as not to demand fulfillment from others. Your goal is to share love, not dole it out as a bargaining chip.

YOU TRUST EACH
OTHER EVEN WHEN
YOU OR YOUR
PARTNER SPENDS
TIME APART WITH
THEIR FRIENDS.

Loving Relationship

Questions 'n Reflections (QnR)
Learning from Relationship Mistakes

Think through your relationship history, starting from the most recent and working your way back in time. With each relationship, answer the first four questions. Save the final two questions for last once you've journaled through your previous relationships. Don't worry about fixing the problem — simply look for patterns.

What attracted me to this goat? Was it physical attraction, a fun friendship, or was it out of loneliness, financial insecurity, family/social pressures or other reasons?

Why did the relationship end? Were there addictions, jealousies, abuse, money problems, lack of commitment or other reasons? Watch out for *scapegoating*! Include your share of responsibility for its failure.

Was the decision to break up mutual? Who ended it? Did you feel bitter, rejected, disappointed, angry, relieved, happy, grateful or other? Explain.

Did I have unmet needs that I expected my mate to fulfill? If so, did this cause you to feel the feelings from the previous question? Explain.

Growing up, did you feel loved? If not, how did you react? Are there traces of childhood trust issues evident in your adult relationships? If so, explain.

What common patterns (or threads) do I detect throughout my relationship history that might be sabotaging my quest for love?

Step 2: It's Time to Grow Up
Stop the Drama Queen Act!

Teach your goat to dance. Get him to stand on his hind legs with a reward. When he does, lure him to turn with another reward. While training him, play the same music and repeat the word "dance." With some practice, you've got a dancing goat.

Learning to cha-cha is great fun, but in real life what happens *off* the dance floor is what matters. Do you find yourself stumbling around in unsuitable relationships, stepping on each other's hooves (drama/trauma) but wishing for more grace and finesse and, above all, a better partner? If so, let's take a look at *why* you are attracting the wrong types that bring out the drama queen in you.

From Step 1, did you discover recurring trust issues? This was true in my case. I chose unsuitable (and abusive) mates over and over again because I *acted-out* from my first betrayal. Reflecting back on that first relationship, I remembered him as a nice upstanding goat from a good herd with respectable community ties. At the tender age of eighteen I gave him my heart hoping he would return my love. My hopes were destroyed when later I discovered him to be unfaithful.

Humiliated and hurt—CLANG—my heart clamped down. That's when I lost touch with who I was. Self-respect diminished and trust faded; I was an empty shell craving more of something to complete me. From then on, I covered up the emptiness with drama/trauma. I buried the memory by setting myself up with future unsuitable mates as my scapegoats with this mantra: *If the so-called nice ones are cheaters, I might as well go for the baahd ones. At least I know what I'm dealing with and I won't be disappointed.*

Subsequently, my patterns of doomed romances and trust issues took hold as I hid behind my insecurities. Back then, I eagerly jumped into any random relationship playing out the role of a victimized drama queen pushing back love. That is, until I tired from these encounters, gave up and grew up. What I gave up was misery. What grew me up was resolving *my* issues (expectations) and resurrecting *my* self worth and *my* trustworthiness.

> **_Trustworthy:_** *Exemplifies emotional maturity. One who accepts responsibility for their behaviors and, when out of line, apologizes quickly and follows-up with rightful action.*

In healthy relationships there is little sign of drama/trauma. They are built upon a solid foundation of honesty, trust and understanding. To attract a healthy and loving relationship, you must do the work to exemplify those attributes you desire in others: honesty, trust and understanding.

In unhealthy relationships, there is no anchor against the storms of life. Until underlying issues are resolved, *buttons* are left dangling and daring to be pushed. And, sure enough, when someone inadvertently brushes up against another's emotional triggers, destructive overreactions occur; trust is tossed to the waves, and so is love. Even the most suitable matches are doomed without the chance to grow.

Julie and Jason had been dating for a few months. Even though Jason was faithful, Julie had trust issues and was constantly interrogating him on his whereabouts. He did all he could to reassure her of his loyalty and trustworthiness until his patience wore thin. While away on a trip, Jason called Julie as soon as he arrived at the airport. During that conversation, he told her he would call her later before bedtime. But when the time came to call, he had trouble obtaining a cell signal from his hotel room and, consequently, he didn't call.

That next morning, he found a text from Julie: *Too busy to call! You must have slept with someone. Hope she was worth it!* Jason was furious and texted back: *Are you kidding me? I couldn't get a signal.* Julie texted in return: *LIAR!!!!* His response: *I'm done...no more drama!*

This innocent misstep cost them their relationship. Had Julie responded by seeking understanding rather than flying off in accusatory anger, a situation like this needn't have destroyed their relationship. If she were clear of trust issues, she'd be more concerned about *why* he hadn't called instead of jumping to accusations (blaming and shaming).

> **Tip:** Texting is good for things like, *YSIC (why should I care)*. It's not a short-cut for conflict resolution. Read more about *Talk Tips* in Step 11.

In the first Step, you tracked recurring patterns from your previous relationships. Here, you're examining the underlying trust issue from all angles by answering and journaling through the following QnR.

In my case I revisited my first betrayal, really pondering its impact on my heart. At first, I felt guilty for what it exposed about my character. I learned that I unknowingly set myself up for recurring drama because I hadn't done the work of processing through the anguish of my original heartache. Those guilt issues ceased once I unraveled and resolved my issues and changed my behaviors.

As you journal, you needn't concern yourself with all the details. Don't over analyze it; instead, allow your emotional memory tell the tale. Answer the questions as *you* remember it. This is for your eyes only. No one is going to argue if your perceptions and memories are different from theirs. How YOU remember it is all that matters. Ultimately, it's not about *them*; it's about that memory stored in *your* heart.

Key Points
Rules 4 No-More-Drama

○ **Pause and reflect:** Instead of shaming and blaming, take a deep breath and reflect on your emotional reaction by pondering...*Oh, wow. I'm having a strong reaction (anger, jealousy, envy, etc.). This must trigger something from my past. If it were brand new, I would be more stunned and perplexed instead of jumping out of my skin.*

○ **Question without blame:** Ask, *"What happened? I waited for your call."* Or try for another way that seeks clarity and understanding. This way, you're not jumping to conclusions.

○ **Tomorrow is another day:** If you are seething with anger or another destructive emotion, take time to think it through. Say to yourself...*I need to give this more thought. I wouldn't want to say or do something inappropriate that might jeopardize this relationship.* Then, put it to rest for a day. Often, situations and conflicts fade away with the moon's phases.

○ **Seek understanding and resolution:** Acknowledging your share of responsibility for your emotional reaction leads you inward. Do the work to dig out underlying trust issues before they sabotage your love life. If it's a petty squabble, open your heart to understanding.

THE RELATIONSHIP
FEELS HONEST,
ACCEPTING, AND
RESPECTFUL. IT'S
LIKE BEING WITH A
CLOSE FRIEND...
NO PRETENSE OR
PRETENDING.

Loving Relationship

Questions 'n Reflections (QnR)
Hot-Button Triggers

In Step 1, you identified patterns of dysfunction cloaked in drama/trauma covering up a tattered heart. To unmask those hot button triggers, do the work to identify their root causes. Ask yourself:

When did this pattern start? Was it from childhood, during my adolescence, my first love, etc.? Explain what happened. Lead with your heart's memory.

Do I continue to set up these scenarios, replaying drama/trauma and hoping for a different outcome? We yearn for final resolution from painful experiences, but if that is impossible, we replay their memories in present day relationships. If this is your case, explain how you've been reenacting an old wound.

What would I say to the original source of my pain if he/she were here right now? Conflicts from long ago are best left alone; that is, no need to kick up the dirt. But still remains your work in putting to rest its memory. Before letting go (Step 3), you must know what it is you are purging. Writing it out helps to get it out.

Step 3: Knightly Forgiveness
Restore Your Broken Heart

Since Biblical times, these playful and mischievous hoofed and horned creatures were tagged by the Hebrews to cast out our sins ... hence the phrase *the scapegoat.*

When out in those dating fields, it's inevitable you'll lock horns blaming others for not loving you the way you deserve to be loved. So, you wrap yourself around the blues rehashing regrets and resentments. Holding on to anger bonds you to the relationship, albeit in a negative way. Singer Etta James made revenue off this notion when she proclaimed, "*The blues is my business and business is good.*" That's all fine and good if you are snuggling up to the memory of what could have been. But if you're ready to move on in a wholehearted way, it's time to forgive, let go and repair your broken heart.

> **Forgiveness:** *From the ancient Greek word "aphesis" meaning to let go.*

For those acting out from a painful memory, letting go (forgiving) is not easy. Often, there's an elixir of shame and guilt stirred up inside the pain. Poking at that hornets' nest could require protective netting (a trained therapist). When anger is deeply felt and multi-layered, it's because the pain is unbearable. In these cases, removing those layers may require the aid of a therapist. You be the judge. For now, warm up your heart to the notion of forgiveness.

Where there's been physical, financial and/or emotional harm done, you're not the same for the simple reason you didn't deserve it to happen. No one *deserves* to be misused and abused! Yet, the longer you hold on to anger, the more you shame yourself by believing you did something wrong or had it coming. This heap of shameful guilt binds you to painful memories. And if you dared to loosen your grip by forgiving the past and honoring your inner truth (you deserve to love and be loved), you'd be liberated from its nasty hold and set free to love again. This is a huge turnabout as a result of forgiveness.

The act of forgiveness is not about denying your past or condoning the actions of those who *done-you-wrong*. It's more about letting go of its stranglehold upon your heart by remembering the incident in a different way (with emphasis on lesson learned). It's a swap: cold-hearted for wholehearted.

> *"Forgiving does not erase the bitter past. A healed memory is not a deleted memory. Instead, forgiving what we cannot forget creates a new way to remember. We change the memory of our past into a hope for our future."* ~ Lewis B. Smedes, author of Forgive & Forget: Healing the Hurts We Don't Deserve

Forgiveness is not a knee-jerk reaction like it is with anger, shame and guilt; it's a conscious choice. You're apt to consciously choose the high road if you've had enough of the low road (drama/trauma). You took the GoatGal's Pledge by proclaiming, *"I cease placing blame on others."* It's time to choose that high road.

The first step in forgiveness and letting go is acknowledging one's feelings of hurt and pain and its reasons why. This is *your* truth! Discovering your truth is like yanking out the weeds of drama/trauma by its roots (the underlying cause of pain and hurt).

Now, go back to the previous Step's QnR's last question. Read again what you would say if you were face to face with the one who's *done you wrong*. To offset victim role-playing and scapegoating and with that bitter memory of your painful encounter fresh in your mind, redirect the finger of blame and rephrase those accusations. (Ex: *I cheated, I gambled, I stopped loving, I abused, I abandoned,* or such.) Maybe you have done some of these things to others and not realized it. We're not angels.

Upon reflection, I've done to others what's been done to me (acting-out from previous hurts). The more we blame and focus on the past, the more we're at fault for behaving in the same way. Author Herman Hesse said, *"If you hate a person, you hate something in him that is part of yourself."* The more damaged we are, the more damage we do. Ouch! Feel how hurtful, shaming and cold-hearted such an accusation is. Feel how the heart shuts down in defense.

Martin Luther King, Jr. told us the heart cannot love if it is unwilling to forgive. I say, let's open our hearts to forgiveness by loosening our grip on the anger. Reframing its memory is how to temper one's harsh judgments and to restore faith in love.

You've taken the first step by acknowledging what and why things happened the way they did. That's the hardest part. To get you to your goal of forgiveness (and to prepare your heart for love) is to remember the past in a way that rebuilds your heart instead of tearing it to pieces.

It's a bit of a trick—rewriting *how* you remember the past—but it can be done. After tracking your failed relationships and unearthing the original source of pain, it's time to treat the wound with a fresh perspective by replacing victimization with empowerment.

A Knight in Shining Armor Forgives

For help with this, call in a knight in shining armor. What would he/she look like? It can be someone known (male or female), as long as it's someone you admire who shows him/herself as courageous and trustworthy.

For me, I swiped the scene from *Gone with the Wind*

where Rhett Butler grows tired of Scarlett's conniving manipulations. In the end he tells her, "*Frankly, my dear, I don't give a damn.*" I especially liked how he then turned on his heels and walked out of her life, head held high. I related to Rhett and Scarlett's tumultuous relationship filled with dramatic lustful betrayals, reckless behaviors and abuse. I'm drawn to Rhett as my knight because, in spite of it all, he sobered up, delved inward and got right within his own heart. If he hadn't, their story might have ended in a more *Fatal Attraction* sort of way.

Find your own vision to transform your memory in an uplifting way. Glean the knight in shining armor lesson even if it is to simply say, "*Enough is enough!*" Be sure to paint a memorable image in your mind.

Once you get the hang of *how* to remember the past, transform YOU into your knight in shining armor. In this way, YOU are empowered, courageous and trustworthy. Here's how. Work through the following QnR. As you do, visualize the painful memory that caused you hurt and heartache. Now, add to that vision YOU as the role of the knight in shining armor—you who took the GoatGal's Pledge and is ready, willing and able to love and trust YOU—and place her side by side with the vulnerable younger version of you (when that first pain was felt). Visualize your younger self being cared for and nurtured as you wrap her up in your arms. Tell her she is loved and loveable, regardless of how others have treated her. Whisper to her, "*You can trust me, now!*" You might not 100%, fullheartedly believe in this vision at this very moment, but for now, make this a new and reframed memory. In Step 4, you'll surround yourself with love and healing.

"Painful experiences are often best healed by positive ones that are their opposite — for example, replacing childhood feelings of being weak with a current sense of strength. If sadness from mistreatment in an old relationship keeps coming up, recall being loved by other people, and let those feelings sink in. Add the power of language by saying something like this to yourself: 'I

got through all that, I'm still here, and many people love me.'
You won't forget what happened but its emotional charge will
steadily diminish." ~ Rick Handosn, Ph.D. and Richard
Mendius, MD, *Buddha's Brain*

After examining your past heartaches and after making peace
by finding the strength from the lessons learned, be patient and
steadfast. This is a huge step and, most likely, a new perspective in dealing with life's experiences. Keep in mind that old
habits are hard to break. You may find yourself reverting back
to the old ways. When such behavior creeps in, gently remind
yourself (in a knight in shining armor loving way) of your new
commitment to forgive by examining your motives and issues
before judging another's. More often than not, what is *done-to-
us* more often has nothing to do with us. That is, it's not personal; it's more a reflection on the transgressor's issues. Take
some time to relax and breathe through the moment. Easy does
it! Big leaps are not necessary, but steps in the right direction
are.
      If the original source of pain is still present in your life
and causing you harm, you needn't *choose* to be the victim. As
an adult, you are in charge of your own happiness. If someone
mistreats you, stand up for yourself or get help to remove you
from harm's way (contact the police or a women's shelter).
Don't waste another moment accepting another's exploitation,
abuse and unkindness. As previously mentioned, if the pain is
deep and too overwhelming to tackle on your own, seek thera-
peutic counseling to help you move forward.

"When you forgive, you in no way change the past but you sure
do change the future."

~ Bernard Meltzer

Pledge to Forgive

*Through forgiveness and lessons learned,
I release the pain of past heartaches.
Upon self reflection, I realize I am not
a saint. At times, I am at fault for
exhibiting reckless behavior. By making
amends and by adjusting my behavior
with rightful action, I forgive myself
for harm inflicted on others (and myself).
With a mended heart, I am relationship
ready.*

Key Points
Steps 4 Forgiveness

○ **Identify your original source of pain and hurt.** Until you do, you are at risk to act out (drama/trauma) from the wounds of yesterday's heartbreak.

○ **Visualize someone you admire who is trustworthy.** Imagine how that person would have handled your original source of heartbreak. Let him/her be your knight in shining armor even if all he/she does is step in and say, *"Enough is enough!"*

○ **You survived!** Acknowledging the strength it took to endure the past empowers YOU! Now, place her in your memory time-line, nurturing and loving your younger self. Whisper to her, *"You are loved and you can trust me now!"*

○ **Reframe *how* you remember the past**. Lessons learned and wisdom gleaned release your grip on the bitter past by replacing its memory with empowerment. This is the path to forgiveness and, ultimately, wholeheartedness.

YOU UNDERSTAND THAT ANOTHER'S EMOTIONAL UPS AND DOWNS ARE NOT ALWAYS ABOUT YOU.

Loving Relationship

Questions 'n Reflections (QnR)
No More Scapegoating

Hiding behind shame, guilt and anger (and blaming others) pushes love away. To release those obstacles, identify *who* and *why* you must forgive, including *yourself*. Then, script out your reframed memory (lesson learned) as many times for as many painful unhealed memories.

Who have I been blaming for shutting down my heart? Explain what happened.

Are you holding onto shame and guilt due to another's manipulations and control? If so, explain how so.

How have I been acting out in anger and shame? Reflect back on those times you pushed love away.

What have I done that needs forgiveness? Did you tolerate unacceptable behavior? Or, manipulated another into your life for selfish gain or other goatish offense? If so, explain how so.

What lessons have I learned from these experiences? Swapping the pain for wisdom (lessons learned) is how to let-go (forgiveness). Such empowerment lifts the anger and opens the heart. Releasing its stranglehold is how to honor your truth, a path to wholehearted love and trust.

How do I restore wholeheartedness by remembering a past memory in a reframed knight-in-shining-armor sort of way?

If I cannot get past my anger and shame, what am I willing to do to resolve my past? (For example: Seek counseling or support groups.)

Step 4: Increase Your Love Ability
Open Your Heart to Joy and Love

Carl Sandburg, the renowned poet and a Pulitzer Prize winner, was married to a world famous goat breeder. When *Life Magazine* asked him to pose for a photo alongside his favorite dog in 1938, he insisted the picture be taken with his goats instead. He was also fond of singing to the goats in his living room.

There's no data on whether or not Steve Jobs, entrepreneur extraordinaire and co-founder of Apple Inc., was as fond of goats as Carl Sandburg. We do know he was a visionary and mighty successful. He said, *"You can't connect the dots looking forward; you can only connect them looking backwards. So you have to trust that the dots will somehow connect in your future. You have to trust in something — your gut, destiny, life, karma, whatever. This approach has never let me down, and it has made all the difference in my life."*

You've connected the dots by completing the first three Steps. You reflected on what doesn't work—doling out and grabbing love to fulfill unmet needs. Now, let's try something that will work—sharing love in a wholehearted way. Not feeling wholehearted, yet? Then let's create new habits that open your heart to joy and love right now.

Inhale three slow deep breaths and exhale slowly. Next, wrap your arms around yourself and give yourself the tightest hug of your life. Do this right now! Tell yourself, *I love me.*

Louder, LOUDER! *I LOVE ME!* Allow every cell to resonate with the love you unconditionally accept. NO ONE can take this away from you. This love belongs to you. You hold the key. It is safe. Every time you go to bed, wrap your arms around you and say out loud, *I LOVE ME!* When you wake up, do it again. Never forget you are loved by your most loving self!

If you're not buying into the concept of *loveable you*, take a look around and witness love already here. It's bountiful beyond measure. Hear it in the music, see it between two lovers on the park bench, and observe it in the tenderness between a mother and child (or any other heart-tugging moment). Breathe it into your heart. Feel it move through you as a psychic shift. Recount how many times a day your heart is touched by a loving and joyful moment. The more you count those moments, the more they multiply. Tuning into its boundless energy aligns your heart to love's perfect flow like a surfer on a wave propelling you onward. You needn't despair waiting for another to love you—be a part of the joyful love wave right now.

The following are ways to get you *in-the-mood-for-love*. Make loving oneself a daily habit. Soon, your heart will be overflowing with love to spare and share.

"To love oneself is the beginning of a life-long romance."

~ Oscar Wilde

Connecting Your Heart to Joy and Love

- ☯ Open-hearted: Start and end each day with self-proclaimed love and hugs. Be open to the love that surrounds you, even if it's basking in the joy of a bird's morning song.

- ☯ Serenity: When feeling anxious about whether or not love will ever find you, look for ways to connect to the present moment. Quiet your mind and open up your senses. Feel nature's warm embrace! When you notice your worries creeping back in, gently tune into your surroundings to regain a sense of calm. With daily practice, such calming and centering habits create more space in your heart for love.

- ☯ Love letters: Write yourself a letter as though it were from your true love. Write with a flourish, describing all your irresistible traits. Then write a letter to your imagined lover. Describe all those intimate details that only lovers can share. Practice makes perfect for when the moment arrives.

- ☯ Visualize: Make a love-collage on a poster board or any size board and display it where you see it daily. Go through old magazines and cut out images that appeal and connect to your heart. These could be images of couples on a beach, a happy family, a white picket-fenced yard, a kitten or puppy, a baby, or any such image that captures love's meaning for you.

● Random loving kindnesses: Bake a cake and invite your neighbor or friend over to share it. Or help out a co-worker who is overwhelmed with work. Your heart's generosity sets the love vibe in motion.

● Love surrounds you: Pay attention to joyful and loving expressions exhibited by others. Reflect on any changes you might feel. Is your heart more responsive and open to love? If so, write about it in your journal. Make a habit of recording these moments. Use the following QnR to help sort through any shifts in your attitude. Validating those shifts increases your love ability. When the right one comes along, your heart will be ready.

● Transform anger (hot button triggers) into gratitude: Review Steps 1-3 to unravel anger's origins and to release its power. Feel the gratitude (joy) of learning your own truth (empowerment). In this way, you understand more of your heart's desires.

Key Points
Rules 4 Love Ability

- **Nurture self.** Love yourself in the same way you would dote on another. Make nurturing self a daily habit to replenish your energy and renew your love-able spirit.

- **Witness love around you.** Be on the lookout for random moments of love and kindness. It could be any feel-good-moment you witness, whether it happens to you or to someone else. When you find it, pause and absorb that very moment as you etch it onto your heart. Once you get in the habit of expecting these good vibrations, observe how love and joyful encounters multiply. Be sure to embrace each moment, making it a vivid memory.

- **Spread random acts of loving kindness.** Even if it's just a smile and a *thank you,* do it from the inside out. Make each gesture meaningful.

- **Transform anger (a hot button issue) into gratitude.** Chart its course (Step 1). Unearth its origins (Step 2). Seek forgiveness by learning its lesson (Step 3). Bask in the gratitude of discovering your inner truth and your heart's desires.

YOU CAN'T IMAGINE
LIFE WITHOUT THE
OTHER. YOU FEEL
LOVED, CARED FOR
AND RESPECTED.

Loving Relationship

Questions 'n Reflections (QnR)
Increase Your Love Ability

Answer these questions each night before falling asleep. It's best to keep a bedtime journal to instill these good habits.

What did I do today that was nurturing? Examples: Eating well, meditating, exercising, reading a good novel, and other ways that center you and align your heart.

How was I generous (and sharing) in a loving and joyful way? Generosity is not only measured by how much money you donate, there are other ways. Offering your time, lending a sympathetic ear, a warm smile and a gracious *thank you* are a few ways.

Did I do this without expectation (pay backs) or a hidden motive? If not, how can I work to put that expectation aside? It is said that expectations are premeditated resentments. When you do something for someone and they do not receive the gesture the way you anticipate, this sets off negativity simmering inside (anger) which shuts down the heart vibe. To work through those setbacks, review Steps 1-3 to remove those expectations.

Did I witness others exhibiting joyful and loving expressions? If so, what were they? Examples: Love between an elder and their caregiver, children at play, a pet snuggled up next to you, a couple tending to their garden and other numerous loving moments.

How do I know my heart is whole? Describe what it feels like to be on the giving *and* receiving end of love and joy. If you fall short, go back through Steps 1-3 to filter out resentments and restore the heart to wholeness.

Step 5: Who's Your Goat?
Call Up Your Compatible Mate

There are more than 300 breeds of goats; they are considered by some as the most versatile animal on our planet. Some are good for milking, will cut your grass for free, have good hair, can pull a cart, and make great loving companions.

With so many goats to choose from, it's easier to be charmed by a wild buck or drawn into rescuing a mysterious desperado than it is to stay on course for a suitable mate. Attracting a compatible mate is more about *calling up* those qualities compatible to yours than it is about opening the barnyard gate to just any ole goat. And for those who haven't done their personal growth work in aligning their heart, that darn barnyard gate just keeps swinging back and forth without prudence or forethought.

Before conjuring up your special someone, step back and ponder why you want a mate beyond the *oh so addictive* euphoria of chemistry. Some go around seeking a new relationship just to catch a lustful high. As with all highs…crashes follow, the thrill is gone, disenchantment shows up, and love never had a chance (nor was it ever a motive).

What is your motive? Are you really looking for a loving relationship or only a romantic encounter? Be honest! If it's more about the chase than it is an actual loving relationship, examine your unresolved trust issues (Steps 1-3). Assuming you are serious about a love quest, ask yourself *WHY* you desire a special someone. Do you yearn for marriage and a family? Or if your kids are grown and you're looking for a loving travel companion, then set your radar on someone retired and ready to explore the world. Knowing *why* frames the bigger picture. Next, fill in the lines. Paint the canvas by calling up a compatible mate (with attention to details on *compatibility* more than outside attraction). Train your heart to see inside his.

Hilda had an eye for a certain type until Nathan came along. That's when she listened to her heart. After sixty years of marriage, she explains how she knew he was the one.

"Nathan and I worked together in the same office. Initially, I didn't think of him as someone to go out with because he was shorter than me. Quite frankly, the taller ones were more my type. Then one day I observed how he handled a difficult client. He was very patient and understanding. I thought if he could be that tolerant to a cranky client, imagine how caring he would be to one he loves. So I started flirting with him and he asked me out. I sure am glad he did because we've had a beautiful life together. I can't imagine my life without my Nathan. He's heads above the others!"

I hear you bemoan, "*But I need chemistry. I must be attracted to him before going out with him.*" I agree, you can't expect love to blossom without chemistry, but you can set your attraction-radar on a heart of gold underneath the outer shell. Good looks fade in time, but a good heart lasts forever.

Don't date beneath you...set your standards high.

"Since you are 'in the market' you need to set standards of what you are seeking in a partner and in a relationship. Dating is not simply a prelude to a committed relationship or marriage. Dating is an opportunity to evaluate whether the person you are dating is a good candidate for YOU. You need to pay attention to your partner's positive and negative characteristics. Ask yourself whether you could live with this person for the rest of your life."
~David Price, *Finding a Lover for Life*

Too often we hear horror stories about scammers preying upon his or her victim under the pretense of love. Once gone, so was the bank account. Don't be a patsy! Set your standards high by aligning your heart with another who also has high standards — honesty, loyalty, trustworthiness, etc. They are your benchmarks. Detecting these qualities takes a while, but the investment of time is well worth it. Your watchword is: *Vetting* (not petting)!

Setting standards is paramount, but don't confuse this with perfectionism. Within all loving relationships, there are compromises that smooth the outer edges in each of us. In truth no one is perfect, not even YOU. I am not advocating you ignore his behaviors. His actions reflect his character, the same as what you do reflect yours. It does matter if he's considerate of your feelings and shows himself to be trustworthy, but if he enjoys bicycling more than gardening, that needn't be a reason to toss him away. You desire a compatible mate who respects and loves you as you do him, in a deeper way that outshines petty differences.

Is your dealbreaker list sabotaging your dating success?

When on a date, are you preoccupied over your dealbreaker list, silently checking off why he is an unlikely candidate? Do you more often attract those you *don't* want? This could be your way of pushing love away. If this rings true, review Steps 1-3 to be sure you aren't holding onto burdensome baggage. Then, tweak your focus. Look for positive attributes instead of negative ones. For example: *No drunken gamblers* rephrased as *health conscious and fiscally sound* shifts your radar to what it is you *do* want.

Walk the talk. Exemplify those standards you seek. Be the lady a gentleman seeks. Align your heart's desire to *your* standards. Do what Hilda did; call up a heart of gold…nothing less will do.

Key Points
Rules 4 Calling Up Your Mate

- **<u>Define your long-term goal</u>.** When on love's quest, look beyond the initial attraction stage when defining what you desire. Knowing *why* you are seeking a compatible mate—companionship, marriage, a traveling partner, etc.—sets your love vibe in motion for the long-term.

- **<u>Set standards</u>.** Identify those things about yourself that you value (your standards); that will help you recognize similar traits in a compatible mate.

- **<u>Turn dealbreakers into dealmakers</u>.** To attract what it is you *do* want, stop thinking about what you don't want. Set upon your love quest on a positive note: *I'm interested in attracting a mate who is ready to settle down and rear a family*, instead of: *I can't stand all these losers*. What you focus on is what you attract.

- **<u>Tune into your heart's desire</u>.** Seek compelling attributes (beyond physical appearance) that will pass the test of time. Listening to your heart's desire is how to align your heart to his.

YOU KNOW EACH
OTHER'S FAULTS
BUT YOU OVERLOOK
THEM WHILE
FOCUSING ON
ONE ANOTHER'S
ATTRIBUTES.

Loving Relationship

Questions 'n Reflections (QnR)
Call Up Your Mate

A loving relationship is your goal, but frustration sets in when the finish line is blurry. To plot the journey, look less "out there" and more inside yourself to help conjure up what it is you are seeking and why. Ask yourself:

Why am I seeking a compatible mate? Beyond the thrill of attraction, what do you want? (Ex: marriage, a companion for travel, etc.) If there are hidden ulterior motives not aligned with your heart (i.e., neediness, desperation, etc.), this could be a stumbling block (Steps 1-3).

What are those standards, compatible to mine, that I look for in a mate? When you meet him and recognize those traits in one another, your hearts will connect.

What are the dealmakers I look for in a mate? Focus on the positive (dealmakers), not the negatives (dealbreakers).

Other than physical traits, what would I find attractive in a mate? Seeking qualities that outlast the passage of time is how to train the eye to look deeper.

How would I describe myself in ways not having to do with outside appearance? Perfectionism is expected of athletes but not in matters of the heart. Include shortcomings as well as attributes as a way to squelch unrealistic demands on self and others.

How would I describe my compatible goat with less emphasis on looks but more on how my heart is aligned to his? Visualize him in your life, but see him through your heartfelt senses. Describe those compatible qualities that define the one you want to grow old with.

Step 6: Are You in a Rut?
Release Your Aphrodisiac

When the goat is in a "rut" he eats less, is stinky with a foul musky odor, and can't resist a doe-in-heat. He'll curl his lips and urinate on his forelegs and face, spreading his scent to entice the doe.

That's what the bucks do, but we goatgals must come up with a better approach. Innately we're social creatures, but when disconnected from others, we get lonely and resort to desperate measures. To circumvent a hasty roll in the hay (jumping into goat pens for all the wrong reasons), release *your* aphrodisiac (your zest for life) to better your chances of attracting a more suitable mate.

> *Aphrodisiac: An inner glow – your zeal and enthusiasm. It's what impassions YOU! This is your alluring feminine power.*

In other words, stop fretting over *when* he's going to show up and get to work learning *how* to enjoy life which, inevitably, will connect you to others and your special someone.

To shake off that in-a-rut lonely feeling, fill your life with activities that please you and give you a sense of joy and purpose. Reconnecting with that long lost, fun-loving kid tucked and hidden within you allows your inner glow to shine through. Before you know it, you'll soon find yourself back in the groove of having fun and attracting others.

For years, I forgot what F-U-N (**F**ind-**U**r-**N**iche) felt like.

I was too focused on misery and lost the capacity to be spontaneous and joyful. Tired of being miserable and alone, I searched into my childhood and early teenage years (before drama/trauma took hold), trying to remember what I enjoyed doing. It was then that I remembered I had fun playing outdoors with friends and I also loved to dance. So, timidly I signed up for ballroom dance classes, joined hiking groups, and took up tai-chi where I met a variety of like-minded and fun-loving goats and goatgals.

My passions multiplied, and so did my zest for life. Energized, I did more. I joined a local jazz club and became active in organizing gigs and concerts. Substituting loneliness for joining up with others reunited me to ME. As I did, my self-esteem and confidence grew. No longer isolating, I felt more at ease in social settings and became much more interactive and friendly. In no time, my social calendar filled up with dating opportunities.

Whatever your passions (dancing or hiking, tai-chi or star-gazing, political activism or such), dabbling in play recharges you, emitting that *young at heart* feeling. Plus, it eases you into the dating scene, but not in a forced and desperately heated rush.

If you're too timid to join a play group without dragging a friend along, recruit someone to go with you. But it's better to go alone, and it's okay to be shy. A little shyness is normal and this can work in your favor. Going solo, like I did, causes folks to be curious about you and more likely to approach you and welcome you. You may feel awkward at first, but try to go at least three times in a row before deciding if this is for you. By the third time, you'll be a "regular," welcoming newcomers.

The more you nurture your playful spirit and the more you fall in love with those things that give you purpose, the more relaxed, confident and authentic you become. It's your feminine power. The passion that drew you in becomes the aphrodisiac that draws others to you. Your dynamic self is what makes an alluring impression, much more than any physical attribute. Here's why, from a male cousin of mine:

> "In the beginning, there was chemistry and I found her attractive, but so are hundreds of others. I fell in love with her because she was genuine…not fake. I felt good being around her. She knew who she was and exuded confidence which put me at ease. The more I got to know her, the more I wanted to please her and to be a better man. I didn't feel I was in competition with her, as though she had a barrier up or that she played mind games. Many women are on the defensive, maybe because they aren't sure of themselves, but she wasn't."

Knowing who you are without pretense is hugely appealing to the male. This puts him at ease so that he, too, can be himself. And let's not exclude that friendly and playful smile which initially captures his attention.

"Love is the very essence of your being. Your objective is to ask love within you to make its presence known, to have an awareness of being so full of love that this is what you have to give away. By doing just that, you'll attract more of what you're giving away."

~ Dr. Wayne W. Dyer

Key Points
Rules 4 Releasing Your Aphrodisiac

- **Add fun to your daily routine.** Love, work and play are three important elements of a balanced life. When one element is missing, at least you have two others to fill the gap until you fill in the third. So, taking time out of your schedule to pursue playful activities is as vital to your sense of well-being as a productive work ethic and a desire for a love connection.

- **Be child-like.** To shake off a rut, lighten up! Reconnect with your playful side by remembering what it is you enjoyed doing in your younger days and set out to pursue those fun times. If hopscotch is no longer your cup of tea, take a trip to the lake. Learn to be in the moment. That's where all the fun is!

- **Do something new.** Try out a new interest or simply go somewhere you've never been before, even if you must go alone. An adventure freshens your perspective and delights your senses. And when that chance encounter happens, you'll have interesting and fun topics to talk about.

- **Join an organization.** Enlarge your circle of friendships by becoming active in your community doing those things you believe in. It's a way to enjoy new acquaintances and like-minded folks and to feel purposeful outside your work environment.

FLIRT

GO ALONE TO A PARTY
INSTEAD OF RUNNING
WITH A HERD OF
FRIENDS. THIS WAY,
YOU ARE MORE
APPROACHABLE.

Questions 'n Reflections (QnR)
Release Your Aphrodisiac

I often hear males complain about females who run in a pack (or herd). They find it intimidating and often are less inclined to strike up a conversation. With that in mind, find ways to gain confidence (and make it easier for goats) without using your friends as a security blanket. Adding fun to your life by tapping into your passions gives you a boost of coolness. This releases your aphrodisiac. It's the magic elixir in getting your groove on. Ask yourself:

What are my passions (interests)? List at least three. (Ex; learning a foreign language, basket weaving, tennis, two-stepping or attending film lectures.) If you can't come up with at least three interests, ask yourself: *Who do I admire and why?* What you admire in others is what you seek to possess. It could be someone famous or someone you know. (Ex: an actor you admire—join an acting class or local theater group; a poet—join a writer's group; musician—help promote local talent; an adventurer—sign up for group trips.)

How and when do I intend to pursue these interests (even if I must do it alone)? There's no better time than right now. Start looking around for those opportunities and sign up today.

After at least three attempts to pursue an interest, how did it go? Do you feel any different...less in a rut? Did you meet anyone interesting? Do you feel connected to a group of like-minded individuals and, more importantly, do you feel more connected to YOU? Explain.

Step 7: Dating Guidelines
Or Wear a Chastity Belt

If you are looking to harness a goat, pick one that is of sound mind and body. And NEVER tether a goat. Doing so leaves them prey to wild dogs and other bitches.

Long ago, when your ancestors were churning goat milk into butter, courtship etiquette was rigidly observed. Back then, an unmarried goatgal seen with a potential suitor (without an escort) was snickered at and gossiped about. Those were the days when it was unheard of to date just any ole buck in the field. It had to be someone known, someone whose herd was in good standing with notable barnyard affiliations. Even so, a proper introduction consented to by the elders was the protocol before stepping out on a proper date.

These days it's catch as catch can, and many a potential suitor is of the unknown variety and without references. To help guide you through the ins and outs of dating in today's world with your...*ahem*...integrity intact, here are four simple rules:

Rule 1: Size up your prospect.

Say you met randomly at a party, nightclub or online and he's pressuring you for your number...do you give it to him? Not if it doesn't feel right and if you're getting a creepy vibe. You needn't be concerned about hurting his feelings. He'll move on to another target.

But, let's say you feel a spark of attraction and he's not pressuring you and there's no creepy vibe. Then do you offer him your number? That's entirely up to you, but before you accept a date with someone with whom you have no mutual associations to validate who he says he is, *size him up* first and then decide if he's worth your time.

Explore what type of person he is (beyond the outer layer). Most importantly, get to know *who* he is. As you do, look for those things you two have in common. It could be similar interests or comparable career fields or whatever else that bridges a connection. Unearthing that golden nugget — that commonality — gives you both something to focus on other than the nervous jitters of what to talk about.

Next, capitalize on a common link by chatting it up with follow-up questions that might point you to a mutual acquaintance. (Learn more about the art of chit-chat and how to be friendly — without being nosy — in the following Step.) If there is a mutual association, keep this mental note as a reference — someone to vouch that he's who he says he is. Do what it takes to ensure he's dateable: Not *someone the cat dragged in*, not married and not *on-the-lam*.

Not all chance encounters will lead you to a mutual acquaintance. But there are other ways to get to know more about him as in the case of Joanne and Tom. Joanne met her future husband online. Initially, her attraction was more inward — not about his body type. She was drawn to the photos of him hiking and kayaking, those things she liked to do, which segued into a friendly online conversation. He told her he was a member of a local hiking group and suggested she join in on an upcoming hike. She did some fact-checking and found out more about his group (which had a website). So she showed up for the hike.

If it feels safe to meet, do so; but if it feels risky, don't. In Joanne's case, she felt safe to meet at a group outing on her own terms. When there are no pressured expectations or unnecessary risks from accepting a date prematurely, it's more about making new friends and having fun. In this way, she began *sizing him up* by observing him in real life situations around others.

Rule 2: Wait for him to step up to the plate...get him to do the asking.

Grandma would tell you never to do the asking. Reason being, males value a challenge. If it's too easy, he's less invested. It's the female's role to challenge him while at the same time convey that she finds him interesting (in a flirty way but not in a teasing way).

Modern goatgals might argue against this old-fashioned philosophy, but I adhere to it after testing what doesn't work. (Permit him to open the door, too.) If he can't step up to the plate even after you've done your part in conveying your interest, you can bet *he* wasn't interested.

Joanne found Tom fun and easy-going. She felt an attraction, but it took a few more hiking trips to warm up to the notion of being alone together. Once *she* was interested, she began flirting with him in the hopes that he would ask her out. She weaved her feminine power (her authentic self with no pretenses), releasing her aphrodisiac (her passion for outdoor fun) which captivated his interest. Here's what she said:

"He was shy, so I knew I had to reassure him that I wouldn't reject a date with him. When I heard about an upcoming kayak trip and I already knew he had a tandem kayak, I hinted, *'Tom, I sure would like to go on that kayak trip but...doggone it!...I don't have a kayak. Does this mean I can't go?'* A subtle coaxing was all it took for him to suggest, *'My kayak sits two, so why don't you come with me?'* It was the best first date I ever had!"

Tip: A date needn't be an evening of candlelit dining and dancing; it can be casual — an outdoor adventure — as long as it lends itself to one-on-one time.

Joanne adds, "I'm a firm believer that it's best to wait to be asked. This way they are more enrolled in the idea of being with you since it is their idea (or so it seems to them). I tell my girlfriend this, but she makes the mistake of doing the asking, making the plans, and wondering why goats treat her so flippantly."

No matter how independent you are, hold fast to the tradition of courting etiquette. It simplifies things. Then he'll expect (and respect) you to *set the terms*. It's an old song and dance routine—role playing is—and it's been working for generations; just ask your grandmother.

Rule 3: Set the terms...take it slow.

It's his role to do the asking and now it's your role to set the terms by establishing personal boundaries. Once the date is on, remember it's *only* a date and nothing more. You owe each other zilch in return (beyond a courteous thank you). This stands true whether or not he foots the tab. Upon acceptance of a date, he's in the pleasure of your company...*only*. He expects you to queue up those boundaries.

Mind your p's and q's even if you think the date is going great. Giving into sexual intimacy too soon shifts the relationship from *getting-to-know-you* to a whole other paradigm: *What-was-I-thinking* or more aptly, *why wasn't I thinking*! For risk of a crude illustration, you can't easily put Jack back in the box after he's sprung forth...you get my point. A romantic kiss is to be enjoyed, but a lap-dance is risky. If it doesn't work out, it's much easier to get over that kiss than it is to get over the risky consequences and embarrassment of a hasty roll in the hay.

In Joanne's words, "Even though Tom and I hit it off on our first date kayaking, I didn't want to rush into a serious romance too soon. Before I met Tom, I learned my lesson the hard way. In my previous relationship, I thought it was love at first sight. He was a charmer and I fell for it. We became sexually intimate early on. Later, I found out he was seeing his so-called ex all the while he was seeing me. I felt humiliated. I felt betrayed. I felt jealous rage. It brought out the worst in me.

"I didn't want to make the same mistake with Tom, so I told him I wanted to take it slow. I was prepared for him to get angry. If he had, that would have ended our friendship. He didn't. In fact, he took my hand and reassured me that it was okay with him, too. Quite frankly, I think he was just as relieved as I was. It seemed to put both of us at ease to allow the relationship to grow in a natural way. And, yet, the sexual desire was there between us, which kept us drawn to each other. Holding out on sex was quite sexy…more so than jumping in bed too soon."

Goats are sexually driven. Expect the issue of sex to pop up, and when it does, be clear without bruising his ego or completely rejecting his sexuality. Assuming you are sexually attracted to him, simply say that you find him appealing (which you do) but that you aren't ready (which you aren't). He may test your resolve, and you may have to tell him *no* more than once or twice.

If he ignores you and continues to pressure you, he's disrespecting you (signs of an unhealthy abusive relationship). And if he storms off, it's not a rejection of you; it's more about the fact that his motives were predatory.

But if he's enrolled in the notion of capturing your heart, he'll respect your wishes, admire your integrity and desire you more. As though the gauntlet is tossed and the challenge is on, he'll set out to win your trust. He'll show you what he's made of, impress you with his accomplishments, and find ways to align your heart to his.

Rule 4: Keep your options open until love and trust are set.

When dating someone new, one of the huge mistakes many of us make is to focus only on that one prospect, excluding all others and ignoring friendships. Such undue pressure placed on that potential someone to be your mate (and your whole world, for that matter) can be the kiss of death before the relationship has a chance to form.

While cloud nine hovers over your sensibilities, stay grounded, stick to your routines, make time for friends and family and, by all means, date others if you so desire. While in the early stages of a relationship (no less than three months, but it could be much longer), and no matter how sure of a bet you think he is, don't make life-altering decisions: Don't invest in property together, pay off his debts, move in, get engaged, or other such dramatic decisions based on a titillating new romance.

Joanne recalls: "Tom and I didn't marry until about two years after our first date. I am so glad we took our time without the pressures of getting too serious too soon which only gets complicated and messy and feels forced. Those fun times we shared in a light-hearted and carefree sort of way blossomed into a deep loving and lifelong relationship."

For you, it may take less or even longer than it took Joanne. Every relationship is as different as thumb prints. Once the charming outer veneer is unmasked and when the realness of who he is and who you are (shortcomings and all) peek through, compatibility is revealed beyond the first blush.

"There are two kinds of sparks, the one that goes off without a hitch like a match, but it burns quickly. The other is the kind that needs time, but when the flame strikes...it's eternal, don't forget that."
~ Timothy Oliveira

Online Dating Tips

Be smart about dating a mysterious stranger by playing it safe with these smart tips.

- ☯ <u>Protect your identity</u>: Do not post your personal information in your profile such as your real name, phone numbers, home address, place of work, private email addresses and such. Do not give away personal contact information until you feel it's reasonably safe to do so. It's best to create a secondary free email address for your online correspondences.

- ☯ <u>Do not rush or feel pressured</u>: No need to answer your "hits" right away or feel obligated to answer all of them. Only answer the ones that look promising and offer compatible interests and backgrounds, those things beyond physical attraction. If your prospect is pressuring to meet you too soon or obtain your phone number, put the brakes on. Proceed only when YOU feel comfortable.

- ☯ <u>Phone contact</u>: After you and your prospect have enjoyed online interactions, you might want to speak over the phone, but only if it feels right. You set the terms, though. Tell him when is a good time to call and how much time you have to spend on the phone. Keep the first few conversations short and sweet. Leave him wanting to hear more and vice versa. If it goes well, this may be a precursor to meeting face to face.

♻ <u>Face-to-face meeting</u>: Only agree to meet someone whom you have established some sort of a mutual connection beyond physical attraction. For the first get-together, meet at a public location—a coffee shop or a group activity that you both share an interest in. This way, you are under no pressure to spend too much time together. If the vibe is good, you can advance to a lunch or dinner date at a later time. Wherever you choose to meet, be extra cautious as you would with a complete stranger (because he is). Have your own transportation. Do not get into a private vehicle and do not agree to go to a private home or other private location. As a precaution, let your friends or a family member know where you are going. Do not leave your personal items (purse, drink, food) unattended.

♻ <u>Long-distance meeting</u>: If you are adventurous and decide to hop on a plane to Timbuktu, never agree to stay in your date's hotel room or his home, no matter how optimistic you feel. Make your own reservation (keep it private) until you feel safe and secure.

♻ <u>Internet scams</u>: Online dating opens you up to scammers and imposters (some are posing as military officers and other distinguished professionals included with profile photos stolen from the internet). Beware! If your prospect sends you a money request, a good luck or bad luck "story" that asks for your help, a request for your private information, an urgent request for you to respond immediately, etc., it's a scam or in some way risky. If it feels weird, rushed or pressured, be wary. Do not take any chances—block him!

♻ <u>Profile picture</u>: Submit a current photo (not one taken a decade ago). You needn't invest in a glamorized make-over image that doesn't reflect how you would appear on a coffee date. Resist the urge to be cheesy by showing too much cleavage and leg as this will attract the wrong type. Avoid cropped images of your previous boyfriend's arm around your shoulder.

○ Profile description: There's a saying, *"Less is more."* With that in mind, describe yourself in an engaging way without giving the whole package away. Give them something to fish for. Be honest about your age and relationship status. Include a special interest or hobby. A touch of playfulness is an attraction. Show your feminine side by including something like, *"As much as I like to laugh, I enjoy a romantic quiet mood, too."* If religious or political affiliations are your priorities, indicate such by articulating your requirements in a positive and upbeat way.

○ Size him up: Do your research on your prospect's credibility. The more you know about him, the better you can judge if he's a viable candidate. Find ways to validate he is who he says he is. Ask direct questions about his work, interests, hometown and such that corroborate his profile description. If he's not forthcoming or evades your questions, he's hiding something.

Key Points
Rules 4 Dating

○ **<u>Size up your prospect</u>.** Watch out for wolves in sheep's clothing! Other than his good looks, find out more. Whether you are face to face or on an online social network site, look for things in common (preferably a mutual acquaintance to reassure you he's who he says he is). Then, do some fact checking on your own. The more you know, the less the risk.

○ **<u>Wait for him to ask you out</u>.** It's okay to offer a hint of a suggestion to reassure him that you are interested, but don't do more. If he's truly interested, he'll ask you out. If he's not interested and you do the asking, he may go along for the ride, but you may find out down the long and winding road that he was never emotionally invested.

○ **<u>Set the terms</u>!** Introducing sexual intimacy often cheats you both out of the time to simply enjoy getting to know one another without the pressures that sex brings into the equation. When the chemistry is stoked, set your boundaries. Articulate what those terms are before misunderstandings occur.

○ **<u>Keep your options open</u>.** Until love and trust are set, you needn't become "exclusive" too soon. It takes time before the charm of a new relationship wears off and the realness of one's character reveals itself. Until then, date others and allow him to do the same.

HE DOESN'T PRESSURE
YOU FOR SEX AND
RESPECTS YOUR
WISHES TO HOLD OUT
UNTIL YOU ARE READY.

Loving Relationship

Questions 'n Reflections (QnR)
Dating Guidelines

Beyond that first *"hello"* and until *"I love you forever,"* there's much that can go right and much can go wrong. *Rules 4 Dating* is a commonsense guide helping you navigate through the ins and outs of today's fast-paced dating scene. Ask yourself:

What are the criteria I look for in sizing up my prospect?

How do I plan to safely get to know someone new whose background is initially unknown to me?

Have I typically been the one to initiate a date? If so, explain whether or not that strategy has worked.

When the sexual attraction is strong, how do I set my boundaries so there are no misunderstandings, regrets or resentments in the heat of the moment?

Am I good at keeping my options open until I know he's the one, or do I jump in too soon before trust is set? Explain.

How do I define trust? It helps to identify those trustworthy attributes you possess as a way to measure how keen you are in recognizing it in others. If you haven't experienced a romantic loving *and* trusting relationship, describe other relationships that felt loving and trusting i.e., parent/child, friend/friend, etc.

Step 8: Flirting Finesse
Get Him to Ask You Out

When the female goat is in heat she wags her tail at the buck, which is called *flagging*, **and runs away until she determines the time is right.**

From working through the previous steps, you're relationship ready, you've resolved thematic patterns of dating dysfunction, your heart is whole, and you've discovered the real you—your feminine power. Now, it's time to flirt and get him to ask you out. It could be a chance encounter at the post office or a proper introduction by a mutual friend, but it's up to you to send off a flirty vibe beyond flagging your tail. If you don't engage him (get flirty), he might assume you aren't attracted to him. If you are a wee bit timid about the notion of flirting with someone new, take a lesson from Martita.

"Had I known that day five years ago would be the day I'd meet my soul mate, I'd have been nervous. I was totally caught off guard. I was rushing around after work and needed to mail a package before the post office closed. There was a huge line and I was fumbling around with my keys, my purse and my package," she explained while gesturing to indicate the size of what she needed to mail. "And the last thing on my mind was a chance encounter.

"I literally bumped right into him. The box was so cumbersome that I couldn't see him. He might tell you I did it on purpose, but, scout's honor, it was an accident. He was so HOT! I nearly froze speechless like I usually do at parties and clubs when I'm face to face with someone I'm attracted to.

"While apologizing, I ended up dropping the box and my keys went flying out of my hand. He and I both bent down at the same time. I grabbed my keys and he grabbed the box, insisting on holding it for me while we waited in line together. I spent the rest of the time talking about why this time of day the post office lines are usually long since most people, like me, work and have no choice but to wait in lines and…blah, blah, blah…that sort of thing.

"I noticed him glancing at my return address on the package. Turns out he and I are neighbors, only one street apart! He told me that he moved there a month ago and that he really liked the neighborhood. I told him I liked living across from the park where most evenings after work I walk my dog. He said he would like to join me if that would be okay. So, we agreed to meet around six that same day. All this happened within those fifteen minutes standing in line.

"While driving home, I wondered whether or not he was telling the truth. Was he really a neighbor, was he married, or was he some rapist? You can't be too cautious these days.

"Suspicions aside, once home I changed clothes and grabbed a leash, snapping it on Dudley's collar. After crossing the street with my mighty protective terrier, Louie was already there talking with Milena and Nolan, who live two doors down. Turns out, they knew each other. I found out he and Nolan work at the same office! I have to say, I was relieved he wasn't such a mystery man after all. Later that evening, I called Milena to clue me in on him. What she told me was all good.

"During our outings at the park, I felt a great connection. Not only was he someone I was attracted to, but I really liked his personality. He wasn't pushy, either. For a while I thought he liked me only as a friendly neighbor given that he hadn't asked me out or tried to put the moves on me. Then one day, about two weeks later we got to talking about restaurants and he asked me which one was my favorite. That's when he invited me to go out. I accepted and, well, we had a great time.

"Once we were more seriously dating, I asked him,

'What took you so long to ask me out?' He told me he was totally into me at the post office — it was my smile that got his
attention — and he liked that I was easy to talk to, but he didn't
want to come on too anxious for fear it would scare me off. So,
he gave it time to let me get to know him better."

Was it fate that these two were destined to meet that day
in the post office or did Martita's gift of gab and friendly smile
play a hand? I say, it was a bit of both...fate and flirt. When
fate steps in unannounced (as it always does), be flirty. Show
him you like him, but not in a teasing way as though you are
hitting on him.

Teasing is a manipulation with sexual overtures insinuat-
ing that you are giving it away for free. When he catches on
that it was only a ploy for his attention (and not for sex), he
slithers away feeling tricked and turned-off. Teasing comes on
fast and ends just as fast.

Flirting is more subtle but longer lasting. Eye contact, a
smile and friendly banter capture his attention, but not in a
lewd way. Let him wonder what more he might discover behind those flirty eyes and that alluring smile. As in Martita's
story, she smiled at him and mixed in casual conversation. If
there's some chemistry, he'll enjoy the encounter and wonder
how to keep that good vibe going.

Rule 1: Smile and Ask a Question

It's more often the female's role to do the work in striking up a
conversation. Reason being, a respectful male is watchful of a
female's personal boundaries. Of course there are goatish rams
who barge through to lay their hooves on those who will allow.
Such seductive types you want to avoid.

To break the ice, a friendly smile and eye contact followed up with a question is all it takes to set a goat at ease.
Start off with something simple that has to do with what's going
on right then and there: *"Great band, don't you agree?"* or *"Nice
party! How do you know the host?"* or *"Gee, do you think we'll ever*

get out of this line?" Nine times out of ten, he'll respond. Most goats enjoy talking to a friendly goatgal. But if there is no response or if he's curt, give it up. You don't want to waste your flirt on a deadpan.

Or, say you're at the appetizer table, you could ask, *"My favorites are these stuffed mushrooms, what's yours?"* Don't worry about sounding corny or hokey. Anything will do; it's chitchat, not a formal State of the Union address. If there's a friendly response, counter back. You can make a game of it by asking him to rate the other appetizers. Keep it fun, nothing serious. Don't try to outwit him, just be playful.

You happen to be sitting next to a potential prospect on the plane. (I have a friend who met her future husband on a flight.) After you stash your tote and before grabbing a magazine say, *"Aren't you relieved I haven't a toddler on my lap?"* Smile at him so he knows you are friendly. He might laugh and agree or he might share with you about his last flight when a baby didn't stop crying. Which ever way he responds, keep up the repartee. For instance, *"Seems this row is kid-free. We're in for a serene flight unless your seat partner doesn't stop jabbering. Ha!"*

Small talk is called *small* because it's not a long, boring one-sided monologue. If you notice his eyes glazing over or he's glancing at his watch, you've talked too long. Short quips are best. Each comment should last no more than a minute or less. Offer just enough to awaken curiosity. If your prospect shows interest, he'll ask questions and offer comments, too. Your objective is to encourage pleasant and courteous (never crude) dialogue.

Rule 2: Look for a Common Bond...a Connection

Once a friendly rhythm is set, a more engaging interaction might emerge from striking a familiar chord—a common bond. In Martita's case, standing in line at the post office was their connection (and plus, he was holding her package) which led the conversation to other commonalities. They discovered they were neighbors. In your case, it could be frequenting the same coffee shop, knowing mutual acquaintances, places of interest (cities, restaurants, museums, national parks, nightclubs, countries, etc.), comparable jobs or educational backgrounds, favorite sports teams, similar taste in music, movies, or food, etc.

Discovering threads of connections offers insight into one another's lifestyles, but in a non-intrusive way. Once common denominators are found, there's a rapport and a kinship formed. (My friend, who met her future husband on a flight, discovered they both had a passion for golf, which created an instant bond.)

When his interest is piqued and he queries you in-kind, resist the urge to divulge too much too quickly. Be a bit mysterious, yet intriguing. Keep him curious by answering his question without too much elaboration. Then, pause and query along the same subject line with something like, *"When was the last time you were there?"* Bringing the focus back to him sends a flirty conveyance that you are just as interested in him as he is in you.

They say a good conversationalist is being a good listener. While listening, observe *how* he expresses himself. If he shows pleasure (by his facial expression, body language, and tone of voice), you know he is passionate about that particular thing. Impress him that you've been listening by directing comments highlighting those things he enjoys most. (More about body language in Rule 3.)

Inevitably, conversations wind down. When there's a pause and the energy wanes, freshen it up by shifting to another topic. Transition by saying, *"Forgive me for changing the subject, but it just occurred to me that..."* Or, segue into a new subject, *"I'm glad you like mushrooms, too. Not everyone does. What do you think about goat milk? Ever tried it?"* Don't get nervous just because there is a pause. There's more you can do with a bit of flirty body language in filling in the silence.

Rule 3: Body Language Conveys Much

Show him you're interested.   Body language properly exhibited adds that subliminal punctuation mark. It can either send him away or bring him closer. The right gesture shouts — *I've got to get you into my life!* — without having to sing it out loud.

When the conversation rests in a quiet pause, capitalize on the moment. A warm smile, a tilt of your head or even a simple gesture as slowly stroking the rim of your wine glass gets him to wonder what's on your mind. He'll soon get the message.

His gestures express words unspoken, as do yours. A keen observation of his body language reveals much about him. When he's nearly breaking his neck to stare at another's legs, it's a no-brainer that he has tuned you out. But the way he looks into your eyes says plenty, too. Look for hidden indicators as a gauge pointing to the success or failure of your encounter.

Rule 4: Encourage Him to Ask You Out

When the chit chat vibe and body language are positive and you sense a connection, end the encounter in a way that says *call me*. Hopefully, he's already suggested a plan to reconnect or at least he's asked for your number. If not, more prompting on your end is needed before saying goodbye. If he still hasn't shown initiative, then simply tell him you enjoyed the visit and would like to talk again. If he picks up the cue and asks for your number, be ready to hand him your card. If he doesn't ask, offer him your card and suggest he call. Either way, hand him your card! If you haven't a card, then get some printed up and carry them in your purse. You needn't be a CEO of BigBucks-R-Us to have a calling card.

Offering a potential prospect your card and suggesting he call may sound like you are doing the pursuing, but you aren't. It's *encouraging* him to stay connected. He still must step up to the plate, pick up the phone and make a plan. If you never hear from him, consider him unavailable whether from lack of confidence or interest or other reason. I'm not suggesting you hand out your number to every buck in the dating fields. Be discerning and selective; give it out only to those *you* are interested in.

If he offers you his card before you have given him yours, accept it with a polite *"Thanks! But just so you know, I'm not in the habit of calling. I hope to hear from you though."* Then hand him yours. Either way, make sure he has your number and tell him you look forward to hearing from him. Your objective is to enroll him into the idea of seeing you again.

"There are times not to flirt: When you're sick. When you're with children. When you're on the witness stand."

~ Joyce Jillson

Chit Chat Do's

"A man is already halfway in love with any woman who listens to him." ~ Brendan Francis

☻ Do practice the art of chit chat with your niece, your neighbor, your kid's teacher, the waiter and anyone else. Make it a habit. The more confident you become in friendly banter, the easier it will be to engage a potential prospect when the moment arrives.

☻ Do start the conversation with a question about the sur-roundings or events transpiring at that very moment. If the repartee goes well, and if it seems appropriate, intro-duce yourself in a casual way, *"By the way, my name's Peggy."* He'll probably reciprocate by offering his name, so be sure to respond with *"My pleasure, John"* or some-thing similar, but make sure you repeat his name. Include his name again a bit later in the conversation. He'll feel more of a connection each time he hears it. Plus, repeating it more than once helps you remember it. (It's mighty awkward to be talking with someone who introduced themselves and you already forgot their name.)

☻ Do keep it light-hearted and playful, nothing critical or negative. Avoid the subject of politics and religion (unless you are at a political rally or a church social or if such topics are your priority).

☻ Do talk about those things you like. It could be a certain movie, song or favorite restaurant. Be genuine; don't pretend you like what he likes or you'll come off as a tease. A better way (if you aren't familiar with his *likes*)

is to ask him to tell you more. It transmits *I find you interesting.*

❂ Do encourage him to reveal something about himself without directly interrogating him. A simple *what-do-you-mean?* or *who's-your-favorite author* persuades him to open up more.

❂ Do look for things in common. If you are standing in line to purchase a ticket to a concert, talk about other performances you've seen. You might discover that you both have similar tastes. Familiarity creates a bond.

❂ Do pay attention to what he says and add to it even if what you say is summarizing what he said. (Example: *I never knew the sloth was considered the slowest moving animal on our planet. Now I don't feel too bad about placing 27th in my last marathon.*) Do your share in keeping the conversation flowing by sprinkling in something about yourself. An added tidbit could segue into more bantering.

❂ Do know when to allow the encounter to end. Less said is alluring and mysterious. Leave him wanting to know more and wanting to see you again.

Chit Chat Don'ts

"Keep the subject focused on the person to whom one is speaking rather than on oneself is polite."
~ Jay Remer, the *Etiquette Guy*

❂ Don't bore him. Pay attention to his responses and body language. If he's crossing his arms, looking around or checking his text messages, change the subject. If that doesn't work, end the encounter with a polite goodbye.

❂ Don't get drunk and act silly or become overly aggressive. You may have a memory lapse, but he might not. First impressions count the most!

❂ Don't tell crude jokes. Jokes can be risky. You might offend instead of impress. Be memorable, but not in a lewd way.

❂ Don't look for conflict when making small talk. If he brings up something controversial, state your opinion and allow him to do so as well. If you discover you both are on the same page, then agree together. If not, agree to disagree (in a polite way) and find something else to talk about, even if it has to do with the weather.

❂ Don't hold him hostage by cornering him and monopolizing his time. If you are at a network function or party, know when to break off the encounter. He might want to mingle (and so should you). If he's interested, he'll make his rounds and come back to you.

○ Don't gossip and talk about other people in a negative way; instead, show off your smile and appeal by staying upbeat and good-natured.

○ Don't talk with your mouth full of spinach dip.

○ Don't brag or exaggerate, trying to impress. It's a turn-off. Be authentic. You're more approachable this way.

○ Don't be condescending and judgmental by portraying yourself superior. This attitude is a mask of low self-esteem and tends to alienate you from others. If you can't be nonjudgmental, simply listen.

○ Don't ask him out! No matter how excited you are to capture his attention, let him pursue you. Drop hints by saying *"Hope to see you again."* Or *"Let's meet again some-time."* Then offer him your card.

Your Body Language

Lean into him more when he's talking. This shows you are interested in what he says and feeling comfortable in his company. Here are more ways to flirt:

- Lips: Males are fascinated by lips (and other body parts). Staring at breasts is lustful and lascivious, but gazing at her lips is acceptable territory. When face to face, watch his eyes as he scans your face. Observing the nuances of your lips is his pleasure point that won't offend. To enhance the appeal, keep them slightly apart. They look fuller and sexier and, plus, it subliminally signals you are receptively feminine (and open to what he has to say). Tightly closed pressed lips come across as uptight, annoyed or angry.

- Head: Slowly nodding to what he is saying conveys you are in agreement. This builds a connection beyond words. (Fast nodding is more that you are anxious to interrupt.) Slight tilt of the head is flirty which subtly exposes the neck.

- Foot: Dangling your loose shoe on the toe of your foot (hoof) shows you are attracted to him and feeling relaxed and playful. A stroke of your foot against his leg under the dinner table is sexy.

- Eyes: They say the eyes are the windows to the soul. Encourage him to discover your innermost soulful secrets. ***Sexy eyes:*** Look into his eyes and let him peek in yours by maintaining eye contact beyond a casual glance (but not staring). ***Flirty eyes:*** Show him your fun side with twinkling happy eyes. You can do this by thinking of something that makes you happy like the idea of you and him on a date. ***Beguiling eyes:*** Looking into his eyes, then looking down and back into his eyes conveys, *"Come hither!"*

- Gazing: Perusing his facial features slowly (from eyes to lips and back again) in a soft gaze shows him you are checking him out. He'll wonder if you have a sudden fantasy about him.

- Eyebrows: Raising your eyebrows indicates you find what he says interesting.

- Sighing: A deep sigh followed by "yes" or "oh" or "ah" affirms that what he said hit a chord. Include a slow nod and he really gets that you get him.

- Gestures: Mirroring his gestures aligns you with him and says that you both are on the same page.

- Hair: Send out a sensual message. Toss your hair back to expose your neck. If you have short hair, then a subtle stroke of your neck will do. Avoid twirling and playing with your hair too much. It comes across as insecure and nervous.

- Touching: While talking, touch his arm to break the physical barrier. This reassures him that you are connecting to him. Touching his hand is very sensual. It sends a strong message that you are attracted to him.

- Laughing: Laugh if he's funny, but don't overdo it or he'll think you are nervous or too silly. Be sure not to laugh *at* him, or he will lose his confidence. Don't make him the butt of a joke in any way. You want to build him up, not break him down.

- Smiling: A warm smile is welcoming as long as it's real. Don't try to fake it, because you'll come across as insincere. A genuine open smile showing off your pearly whites signals that you are friendly.

- Crossing arms/legs: Avoid crossing your arms or holding tight to your purse in a defensive pose. Instead, keep your body language more open and receptive. You can sit with your legs crossed, but make sure the top leg points toward him instead of away from him.

- Glancing: Look back at him. After having a conversation and when walking away, glance back to send him a wave or just a smile. He'll be reassured that you enjoyed the encounter.

His Body Language

While conversing, is he checking his phone messages and hardly giving you eye contact? Or, is he looking into your eyes, smiling and keeping up his end of the conversation? Here are ways to tell whether or not he's interested:

◊ Facial expressions: Are his eyes attentive? If so, keep up the chitchat. But if his face shows boredom, try a new subject. It could be the topic, not you.

◊ His eyes say it all: Good eye contact, he's confident and interested in what you have to say. Squinting eyes, he's unsure and questioning the moment. If he looks upward or sideways, he could be thinking about you and what you said. Downward, he's ashamed or hiding some-thing. Dilated pupils, he's excited and happy (or on drugs). Closed eyes, more than a blink, indicates there is stress or despair. Inappropriately glaring at your body, he's sexually objectifying you. (Meaning: he's not inter-ested in you as a person, only in your body for his needs.)

◊ Arms crossed: Unless the temperature is chilly and he's shivering, this posture could convey he's defensive, cau-tious or self-conscious. Switch the conversation to something else and notice if his body language changes to a relaxed pose.

◊ Fidgeting with an object (cigarette lighter, pen, his hands, etc.): He's bored. Maybe you've talked too long. Give him a moment to share his thoughts. If he hasn't more to say, this could be that he's just not interested; it's your cue to wrap it up. But if he's handling an object with intent (not fidgeting with it), this could indicate he's reflecting on you or the topic of conversation.

◊ Bouncing or shaking his legs: He's anxious to leave (or has had too much coffee). It's best to cut the encounter short and see if he suggests reconnecting at a better time.

◊ Stiff body posture: He's socially shy and/or feeling inept (or his back is out). Take the pressure off by redirecting the conversation to something else not having to do with him or you. For instance, if you're outdoors and it's a clear night, talk about the moon and stars. Notice if changing the focus relaxes him more.

◊ Tilted head: Tilting the head slightly is a flirty gesture. He's being playful and likes the encounter and hopes it continues.

◊ Body distance: If you lean into him and he backs away, he's keeping his distance. But if you lean in and he bridges the gap by leaning in more, he's following your lead and the feelings are mutual.

◊ Hands on his hips: He could be tired, but it also could signal he's impatient and feeling put out.

◊ Shifting his weight or tapping his foot: He could be feeling a bit tortured and anxious to end this encounter.

◊ Playing footsies: If he touches his foot to yours, he's signaling that he's quite taken by you.

Key Points
Rules 4 Flirting

○ **Break the ice.** It's more often the female's job to strike up a conversation. Be ready to flash a friendly smile and include eye contact with a lead-in question about whatever is going on at that moment. It could be about the rainy weather. Anything will do. Steer away from negative comments, though.

○ **Look for a Common Bond.** While chit chatting, look for similar interests, comparable jobs, favorite restaurants, movies, sports teams and such to make a connection. Then, capitalize on that topic to keep up the friendly banter. He'll feel as though he and you might be kindred spirits.

○ **Body Language Tells Much.** A subtle gesture such as raising your eyebrows while he's talking shows you are interested in what he's saying. Likewise, watch for his cues to know if you and he are on the same page. Don't waste your time if he's constantly checking his text messages. But if his facial features come alive when you talk about the migration of sea turtles, then you found a hot topic.

○ **Encourage Him to Ask You Out.** Convey you are interested even if it is to say, *"I hope to see you again."* This reassures him know you wouldn't reject his invitation to meet again.

FLIRT

IN CONVERSATION, SEARCH FOR MUTUAL INTERESTS, ACQUAINTANCES, OR EXPERIENCES TO CREATE A COMMON BOND.

Questions 'n Reflections (QnR)
Let Him Know You're Interested

Attracting a loving relationship has to start somewhere. An initial encounter with flirty exchanges stirs up chemistry. But if you are having a hard time getting a goat to ask you out, maybe you need to tweak your approach. Ask yourself:

When I meet someone I'm attracted to, what do I typically do? (Clam up, run away, tease, act desperate, etc.) Be specific by recalling your last three encounters.

Looking back on those three encounters, would there have been a better way to signal my interest? If so, explain.

What is my idea of a fun date? Come up with a list of date ideas to hint at i.e., a full moon hike or a swim at the lake sets a romantic mood.

Step 9: Avoiding a Roll in the Hay
A Romp, Quickie, One-Night-Stand

Pan, half-man, half-goat, is the Greek god of the Shepherds as well as the charming seducer of the nymphs. Pan's greatest conquest was that of the moon goddess Selene. He accomplished this by wrapping himself in sheepskin to hide his hairy goat form, and drew her down from the sky into the forest where he seduced her.

A male friend of mine, Dan, makes this confession, "Pan was more infatuated with the art of the chase in wooing and winning over his target like a sporting event. Typical of some males today, including myself. I'm less interested in what occurs after the sexual conquest. In fact, I'm suddenly not interested at all."

Goatgals, be forewarned! Just because he takes your breath away, don't confuse lust for love. Sexual intimacy is not a precursor *for* love, nor does it guarantee love. In healthy relationships, it's an expression of love already formed. Yet when your hormones are spinning, it's hard to say... *No, let's wait!* Nevertheless, it's your responsibility to distinguish whether or not *love is here to stay* or run the risk of *lust is gone by tomorrow*.

Roll in the Hay: Engaging in sex before establishing a loving and trusting relationship. Seemingly consensual, but more of an impulsive sexual gratification often used as a manipulation (a pretense for love or other hidden motive).

Truth be told, females enjoy sex just as much as males but for different reasons. Males initiate it more often for the physical connection. Females do it more for an emotional connection. And when coupled with a foundation of love and trust, it's nirvana. Without those touchstones in place, though, bedding down too soon might send regret and shame to step in when he steps out.

In a scene from the movie *Young Frankenstein,* right after Madeline Kahn gets it on with Frankenstein, she laments, *"Oh, you men are all alike. Seven or eight quick ones and then you're out with the boys to boast and brag. You better keep your mouth shut! Oh...I think I love him."*

All kidding aside, a hasty roll in the hay feels good at that moment. That is, about as long as it takes to light up a cigarette. But the not-so-good consequences could last a lifetime, including an STI and/or an unplanned pregnancy. And then there's the aftermath of the emotional crash from a wounded heart.

Some argue: What's wrong with two consenting adults agreeing to have *no-strings-attached, protected sex*? Nothing, if all you want is sex. Even so, rarely do friends with benefits end on a pleasant note. The beginning is at a perfect pitch, but the last encore could be a twangy off-key country song:...*He left me for the waitress at the IHOP.* All of which delays your quest for love.

Some of us fool ourselves thinking a bit of good sex might pave the way for love. Real love can't be cajoled or manipulated, no matter how good the sex is. Love blooms on its own and in its own time. The following are two cases that clearly illustrate that sex can't buy love.

Case 1: Shawna had a crush on Jacob. Anxious to get his attention and win his love, she seduced him. After that night, she never heard from him. She's left with the memory of a one night stand, wondering if things might have been different if only she had allowed the relationship to take hold *before* rolling in the hay.

Case 2: Paula had high hopes for Ron who presented

himself to be intelligent, good mannered, kind to kids and animals, belonged to the same place of worship, and passionate about the same interests. They enjoyed lunch dates and evening outings. The attraction and chemistry grew in leaps and bounds. She was sure (well, nearly sure) he was her special someone. So she gave in to his advances and entered into a sexual relationship. Soon after, she felt him pulling away. When confronted, Ron told her he's not ready for anything serious. When Paula confessed her love for him, Ron shrugged and said, "*But **I** never told you I loved you.*" Their relationship crumbled when the truth was exposed: Ron only wanted sex and Paula wanted love.

Don't be rushed!

If it feels too soon, too crazy, too exciting or *too* anything, it's your warning sign to slow it down. A male friend of mine shared this, "Good men but bad boys is a very seductive combination. Touch of rogue and a bit of manners. Unstoppable." But stop them you must! Wait until that sudden jolt of euphoria — that druggy altered state of mind that impairs one's better judgment — to settle down before snuggling up under the covers in search for love.

When pressured by him or when the sexual chemistry is nearly impossible to ignore, assess why *you* feel rushed, bewitched, bothered and bewildered. It's not always about his cravings; it's about yours as well. Take all the time you need until you are in love and loved, trusted and respected, safe and secure. Until then, head off to the gym to work off that sexual over-drive.

Just Say "No!"

As previously discussed in Step 7's *Rules 4 Dating*, you must set your boundaries. Whenever there's a sliver of doubt about yours or his intentions, just say, "*No!*" Assuming he's into you for all the right reasons, he'll wait until you say, "*Yes.*"

On the following page are a few warning signs a relationship is heading in the wrong direction. As you read through, you'll note that it's not always the goat who is to blame; goatgals are just as guilty of misusing their sexuality. To honor the integrity of your heart, make your love quest virtuous by examining one's own motives to better detect such hidden agendas in others.

"Roll, roll, roll in ze hay."

From the movie *Young Frankenstein*

It's Heading for a Hasty Roll in the Hay

Love's quest is perplexing enough but when mixed signals get crossed, it's a collision course. If you notice some of the below warning signs, you may want to recalculate another direction.

✷ *He's coming on strong and pressuring you for sex.*
If you were assured of his love and commitment, you would feel safe and not pressured. Set your boundaries. If that doesn't work, block his number.

✷ *Angry over a baahd breakup, you're considering hooking up with just anyone as a way to get over him.*
When enduring the aftermath of a breakup, it's best to chill out. Don't drag anyone else into the mud until the emotional debris from the storm has been swept away. Hanging out with supportive friends is a safer bet.

✷ *He brags about himself and comes off like a slick sales clerk.*
A hard sell is usually a cover-up for a faulty product. He's probably racing against the clock to close-the-deal and get you in the sack before the jig is up. If he's too impatient to allow you time to discover his redeeming qualities, he probably has none.

✷ *You're unhappy in your current relationship and looking for someone to save you.*
He'll sniff desperation, luring his victim to his goat-pen. Looking to be rescued leaves you at risk to another's sleazy motives. It's better to strap on your own life jacket.

○ *He's too flirty with sexual innuendos. You are feeling icky and uncomfortable.*

Run for the hills! He's not even smooth enough to hide his intent. If you fall for this one, go back a gazillion spaces.

○ *Bored, you head out to the nearest watering hole, get drunk and take home a stranger.*

Once sobered up, you discover he's gone and so is your wallet. Here's a better way to shake of the boredom: anything but that!

○ *He doesn't invite you to meet his friends and family, and he makes excuses not to meet yours.*

He could be involved with someone else and stashing you as a secret affair. If he were seeking an honest and legitimate relationship, he would *want* to introduce you and get to know your family and friends.

○ *You thought it was love at first sight so you fell into his arms.* And so did he…with someone else later that evening. Lust comes on in a heated rush. Love takes time to grow.

○ *He makes plans with you at the last minute and often cancels without an explanation.*

Your time is of no consideration to him. All he cares about is meeting his immediate needs, not yours. Wait it out for someone who values your time together.

Key Points
Rules 4 Heading Off a Roll in the Hay

⚬ **Don't be rushed!** Becoming intimate too quickly often sabotages the best chances of a loving relationship.

⚬ **Just say "NO!"** When in doubt, wait it out. If there is an inkling of doubt where the relationship is heading, don't do it. Stay on love's quest and keep your integrity intact until you are certain.

⚬ **Sex doesn't buy love.** If you find yourself second-guessing his intentions and your motives...*Maybe he needs sex to feel a love connection...or...If I don't give in to his advances, he'll leave me for another...*think again. Love doesn't disappear because you didn't have sex. If the relationship is meant to be, sexual intimacy will wait for love's right timing.

⚬ **Don't get too lonely or desperate.** When anxious to find a love connection, it's easy to be swayed into a lustful encounter. Too often, sex without an emotional commitment leads to a low sense of self-worth which thwarts love's quest. Hanging out with friends while pursuing your own interests and passions helps dissipate loneliness. (Review Step 6 if you are in a rut.)

ROLL IN THE HAY

YOU DID IT AFTER
MEETING ON AN
ONLINE DATING SITE.
AFTER A FEW MORE
CHAT SESSIONS,
HE BLOCKED YOU.
KISS THAT ONE
GOODBYE. BAAAH!

Questions 'n Reflections (QnR)
Roll in the Hay Lessons Learned

Think back on your past unloving sexual encounters, those experiences you regret. In hindsight, it's easy to spot those red flags, but when blinded by lustful attraction it's like looking for a street sign in a heavy fog, nearly impossible to see. Nevertheless, there are lessons learned from missteps. Ask yourself:

What were the red flags I ignored that led me on? Was it my crazy thinking or another's crazy thinking or both?

Was I acting out sexually to bury some other emotional distress (a breakup or loneliness)? If so, explain.

Did I have hidden motives in capturing a goat in a heated rush? If so, explain what the hurry was.

Did I confuse lust with love? If so, how do you intend to be more guarded in the future?

Did I neglect (or resist) setting my boundaries? If so, what do you think would have happened if you had?
How did I feel after I realized it was only a roll in the hay?

In the future, when I am in a risky situation, what am I willing to do in setting up boundaries? If you are having trouble in this department, look inward/backward. There may be boundary issues from long ago that continue to play its hand. (Review Steps 1-3).

Step 10: Is It Just a Play-Date?
Don't Waste Your Time

Young goats love to play. Butting heads is one of their favorites, so watch out! Never push the forehead of a mature goat. They will think you just want to play, but someone could get hurt...namely, you.

Play-dater: Unwilling or unable to emotionally commit.

Most singles unanimously agree that meeting an exciting new mate is their number one goal. Even so, not everyone is looking for the same thing for the same reasons. Some, like you, wish for a loving relationship and others are only interested in a roll in the hay or play-dating – *nothing serious, but sure do enjoy your hospitality, ma'am.* The difference between a roll in the hay (casual sex) and a play-dater is subtle but distinct. The roll in the hay is *only* about a sexual conquest; a play-dater isn't necessarily seeking a sexual conquest (although that could be part of it). It's more about stringing another along without the slightest hope of a commitment, like going along for a ride just to pass the time.

Perfect example of a relationship with no potential is how Rob described his last weekend's date: "We had a good time...dinner, dancing, and a hot make-out-session." When I asked him when he was going to see her again, he shrugged and flippantly said, "Not sure." Stunned, I asked, "What do you mean 'You're not sure?' Aren't you going to ask her out again?" He explained, "Nah, I don't want to give her the wrong impression. She's really nice, but I'm not looking for a serious relationship. If she contacts me, I wouldn't mind seeing her again, but that's about it."

Maybe she wasn't Rob's type or maybe Rob just wasn't ready for a serious relationship. Nevertheless, he'd oblige her offer if she took the initiative because he's only playing at dating. If you find yourself doing all the asking and planning while he's standing on the sidelines, he's probably a play-dater with no relationship potential.

When dating someone new and you suspect he's play-dating (you're doing more than your share of keeping the relationship together), test it out by backing off. Don't ask him to help you move your refrigerator or any other excuse to see him. Do not text, call, email or knock on his door. Do nothing!

Does he wonder what happened? If not, move on. See how long it takes for him to contact you. If nothing happens and he simply disappears off the face of the earth, then you know it was one-sided. Plain and simple...he wasn't emotionally invested.

Caution! If you weaken and contact him, it might spark things up again, but don't misread his intentions. This could set up an unfavorable pattern, you calling the shots which takes him off the hook, claiming no responsibility for the relationship. If he goes away again and like a yo-yo, you call him up to rekindle the flame, what's in it for you? He might get the impression you're okay with the arrangement, but you desire more—a loving relationship.

And let's say you've been seeing other prospects and out of the blue he surfaces. What do you do? Drop everything and everyone else because he remembered you after a mysterious disappearing act? NO!

But if you still have feelings and hope he's done some soul searching and is revisiting the notion of a serious relationship, simply say, "I wish I could, but I have already made plans. Can we make it another time?" He'll catch on that you're no pushover and that he can't merely pick up where he literally left off. If he's sincere about you, he'll take his place at the back of the line and make his way to prove his good intentions and gain your trust. Don't get your hopes up too quickly. Until you know better, be cautious until he proves himself to be more than a play-dater.

Emotional Commitment: You make each other a number one priority.

How you define *emotional commitment* varies depending on what it is you expect from a relationship. Not all of us are looking to tie the knot. Barbara wasn't looking for marriage, but being in an exclusive and emotionally committed relationship was her goal. That's what she thought she was in until one regrettable wedding she and her boyfriend attended. It was his ex-wife (the mother of his four-year-old Bella) who was the bride. Bella was the flower girl. The nervous groom in his military dress blues and the beautiful bride in full white veil regalia made for a traditional wedding with no surprises; that is, until the drive home. Barbara queried her boyfriend of three years: "Honey, how are you going to handle it when they reassign out of town as always happens with the military. Are you going to be okay when Bella moves away with her mom and her new step-dad?" Ray replied, "I'm going with them."

Barbara nearly jumped out of the car. Once recovered from the shock, she gave him opportunity to backtrack with something reassuring like, *"But I wouldn't leave without you."* He didn't. Instead, he told her, "My daughter is my priority." His message was unspoken but loud and clear: *And you are NOT!* Consequently, their relationship ended.

More interesting to note, beyond the reason for their breakup, is what happened years later. That's when she ran into Ray and asked him how things were and how his daughter was. He sheepishly admitted he never moved away. He never followed his daughter (who moved several times to distant locales with her mom and step-dad). He was merely play-dating.

Sometimes we're caught off guard, but other times the red flags are in our path early on. Ally tethered up with a goat who told her from day one, "Relationships are too much pressure, but I really like you." Her attraction for him overrode his warning as she blindly fell crazy in love, hoping to win him over. Early on, the relationship became sexual without an "exclusive" commitment. Two years later, Ally grew weary and frustrated when his old habit of not calling her for days wore thin. When he would call, he offered no reasonable excuse for his absence.

Finally, Ally reached her breaking point and confronted him. He not only reminded her that he was never interested in a relationship, but he went on to say that he does not and never did love her in the way she wants him to. Then and there, Ally broke up and he walked away without so much as a whimper.

Three weekends later (after not hearing a word from him), she called him asking (begging) to pick up where they left off. "At least he's still in my life," she rationalized to her close friends. They lasted on and off for another year. She and he met randomly, mostly for sexual encounters, until he finally dumped her to pursue another. Six months later, she heard from a mutual friend that he married.

It took Ally time to heal her broken heart, but once she did, she met George. They fell deeply in love. Closing the door on an unloving relationship can open the door for a loving one. And hopefully, it won't take you as long as it took Ally to detect a play-dater.

I've been guilty of *enabling* a play-dater. I held onto the hope that someday he would commit. I hesitated to confront him for fear he would bolt if pressured. I nibbled on the crumbs of a quasi-relationship until my self-esteem eroded. While I fretted over why he was more often distant and wondering if I had done something wrong, the more anxious and desperate I became. Then after he canceled our weekend trip to the mountains (which was all my planning) with an offhanded excuse about work, he stopped calling. My inner voice screamed, *It's over without a final goodbye.* And it was.

In Barbara's story, she drew up a scenario—*are you going to be okay when Bella moves away* — drawing out his confession that their relationship was not his priority. In Ally's case, he dropped a red flag (more like a bomb) by his admission— *relationships are too much trouble*—warning her that he was unable or unwilling to commit for reasons unknown. And in my story, I enabled a play-dater—*I hesitated to confront him for fear he would leave if pressured* — because of unresolved abandonment issues.

Every relationship is different. It may start out casually (similar to play-dating) or jumpstart with romance, roses, chocolates, and I-love-you notes. Then suddenly you're not so sure how he feels about you and you sense it's one-sided. While he recoils from *commitment* like a snake, you cling to *potential.* You think "if only" he would step up, the relationship would be ideal. While time marches on, maybe it's you who needs to step down.

Stepping down is not a manipulation. It's taking a stand to move on because he hasn't given you reason to stay. If he's a keeper, he'll make his way back into your good graces.

But if things don't seem to get back on track and he's sending you mixed messages, then talk it out (more about *The Talk* in Step 11) and/or suggest couples counseling. A professional mediator could reveal hidden obstacles with solutions in moving forward. If the relationship is meant to be, he'll catch on, making you his number one priority. If not, cut your losses and move on.

Warning Signs He's a Play-Dater

◊ From the beginning, he's extra casual about dating you. Once he's got you hooked on the line, he drops the effort completely but often will go along with *your* plans.

◊ He told you early on that he is uncomfortable or pressured by the confines of being *in* a relationship. His reasons could be well-founded...he has commitment issues.

◊ On social media sites, he portrays himself as a lady's man. Eventhough he's dating you, he continues to display photos of himself with groups of other women out on the town.

◊ You've backed off and he disappears.

◊ He avoids having a serious talk about the relationship as much as he puts off a prostate exam.

◊ You're more enrolled in the notion of a relationship than he is. The more you push for it, the more he pulls back.

◊ You doubt his feelings for you because his actions are not consistent with his words.

Warning Signs YOU'RE a Play-Dater

- After chasing him down and once the newness of him wears off, you become bored, looking for more exciting prospects.

- You objectify the opposite sex and think of them as boy-toys.

- You're more interested in what he gives you (meals, drinks, gifts, trips, etc.) than in sharing wholehearted love.

- You're broken-hearted from the past and don't want to be hurt again, so you approach dating in a less than serious way.

- You're bored so you accept a date with anyone and everyone just to fill in the time.

- You're not all that interested in him, but you hang out with him in hopes to meet his cool friends.

- You date other play-daters because you have abandonment issues.

- When it starts to feel serious, you skedaddle because you have commitment issues.

Key Points
Rules 4 Detecting a Play-Dater

Dating should be fun but if it leads nowhere, then it's just a play-date. Here are other indicators.

○ **No relationship potential.** Healthy relationships are built upon teamwork and a mutual effort from both. But if one is less enrolled and the other picks up the ball time and again, it is one-sided.

○ **Emotionally unavailable.** Relationships usually start out as casual dating, but soon after the *getting-to-know-you* stage, they progress to the next level, to a more "exclusive" and serious commitment. Individuals in a relationship make one another their number one priority. Play-daters are unable to move to that next level. They make excuses, skirting around the issue or simply telling the cold hearted truth…that they are neither ready nor able to take that next step.

○ **Lack of mutual respect.** Loving relationships are built upon trust and respect. Play-daters lack respect for the relationship and for their mate. They consider themselves and their mates as *friends-with-benefits*.

○ **Mixed-messages.** Play-daters, at times, are romantic and loving while other times distant and detached. Their actions are not consistent with their words. They often look for a way out to avoid feeling trapped within a relationship.

HE WARNED YOU,
"RELATIONSHIPS ARE
TOO MUCH TROUBLE."
YOU DID IT ANYWAY
AND AFTER 3 MORE
ROMPS, HE TEXTED
YOU: "LET'S JUST BE
FRIENDS."

Roll in the Hay

Questions 'n Reflections (QnR)
Quit Playing at Dating

In the early stages of dating, it's acceptable to view each other in a playful and carefree way. Once the preliminary phase has passed and it's time to advance to the next level, you might hit a "No Trespassing" sign, meaning *Emotionally Unavailable*. Before your heart and time are wrapped up in the promise of love, make sure it's not just a play-date. Ask yourself:

Have you ever loved someone who didn't love you back? If so, explain how you knew your love was not shared.

Have you ever chased him down and later wondered if he went along only for the ride? If so, what will you do differently the next go-around?

If you are currently in a relationship that you are unsure about, what steps are you going to take to help you decide to either let it go or stay and work it out?

Are you guilty of play-dating and/or are you drawn to play-daters? If so, explain how you are going to change those patterns and get more serious about attracting a healthy and loving relationship. (Review Steps 1-3)

Step 11: Feeling Unsure?
Have *"The Talk"*

"Oh, it is only I, the tiniest Billy Goat Gruff, and I'm going up the hillside to eat the sweet green grass," said the youngest billy goat in a small, small voice. ~ Janet Stevens, *The Three Billy Goats Gruff*

Most new relationships start out on a smooth track through the tunnel of love. But you can bet your life savings there will be tiffs up ahead (to be expected in all relationships). How you handle those problems tests yours and his commitment.

> **Tip:** When a relationship has a rough start, it's usually an indicator it's not a match. Think of it like putting a peg into a round hole. It wasn't meant to be.

Assuming it started out sweet but got snagged along the way or if he's sending you mixed messages—he's passionate and other times he's distant—and you're second guessing if the relationship is all it's cracked up to be, it's time to have *The Talk* before resentment builds and spews over into a rage. This helps you both sort through issues in a respectful and civil way. Articulating your concerns while listening to his is a vital attribute in every healthy relationship, whether in its early stages or years later. Best case scenario, you and he are drawn closer together. Worst case, you discover you and he are not a match. It's best to know one way or the other. Otherwise, he may assume you are cool with the arrangement *as-is*.

How often do we hear our friends complain, *"He's so clueless! Doesn't he get it?"* Truth is, males are not good at mind-reading. And they don't often stop and ask for directions. They stay the course, following their *GPS* signals unless they are told otherwise. He expects you to tell him (and not in a rant) when things are off-track. Not doing so is neglecting your end of the bargain in mapping out a healthy and loving relationship.

The worst tactic is icy silence; it's the kiss of death. Your cold shoulder will send him scurrying into his man-cave where it's safe and predictable. He'll venture out only when the full moon has waned. For he's frightened to simply ask — *Is everything okay?* — for fear you'll charge at him in a fury.

To prepare yourself for *The Talk*, compose and write out your concerns as a first step in sorting through the problem. This way, you're better prepared to stay on message. This is not a dirty laundry list of what he does that makes you angry. It's more about sharing how YOU feel and what your needs are. Use *"I"* statements and speak from your heart. Keep it brief and concise in order to minimize the risk of misunderstandings. Memorize the main points — no more than three (otherwise you confuse the issue). If he's serious about this relationship, he'll catch on quickly AND he'll appreciate your guidance in what it is you need from him.

With thoughtful preparation, you are less prone to fly off the handle in a reactionary rage. By keeping your cool and keeping it simple — *let's get serious and work things out or not* — places the issue clearly on the table.

After writing out your talk, practice reading it aloud. Let it resonate through your body. Do this repeatedly until you have it down. Once you are satisfied, tell him you need to talk and tell him how much time you need. Ask him, *"When would be a good time?"* This way you have his undivided attention and he doesn't feel blindsided. If he gives you the runaround and implies there is no good time, that's your red flag that he isn't emotionally committed. But if he is sincere, he'll listen to your concerns.

If after having the talk and confirming it's nothing more than a casual relationship with no future, you can choose to let it fade without fanfare, scapegoating or drama/trauma. It's best to remain cordial, leave on a high note and walk away.

The exception to this etiquette rule is if he's a manipulator, abuser or someone overstaying his welcome. In those cases, just end it; you needn't aspire for the Ms. Congeniality crown.

Whichever way it turns out, it's best to clear the air and know where you stand. Once you gain practice, such healthy communication skills enhance relationships between you and others in all areas of your life.

"Communication leads to...understanding, intimacy and mutual valuing."

~ Rollo May

Talk Tips

- **Get grounded**: When things are upsetting you, it's best to clear the air; but if your emotions are out of control, wait to talk about it until you can state your concerns without blaming and shaming.

- **Call a meeting**: When your thinking is clear, set up a time and place that is good for both of you. Let him know in advance how much time you need. He'll appreciate a structured time frame requiring his attention; otherwise, he's likely to tune out. Keep it reasonably short and to the point.

- **Use "I" statements**: *I feel..., For me..., I think..., I want..., I am..., I need..* Avoid "You" statements that blame and shame (*You did..., You never..., Why don't you...*). Your goal is to get him to open up, not shut him down. Follow the "I" statements with a clear and concise request such as:

  I think we are compatible in most ways that matter, but when we talk about politics I feel we don't see eye-to-eye. Can we agree to disagree and put it to rest?

  I feel great being with you. But when we are apart, I need a text or a call once in a while to keep up the connection.

  I need you to know that I am growing fond of you but I'm uncomfortable when you are hanging out with your ex. It wouldn't bother me as much if I were included in those get-togethers. Is that possible? And, if not...why not?

In the past year that we've been "exclusive" I've felt loved by you and I hope you know how much I love you, but I want more from our relationship. I want us to make plans for a future together beyond an upcoming weekend. Is that possible?

❂ Let him have a turn: Then pause and allow him to speak. In other words, get to the point, tell him what you need and listen for his reply with an open heart. He may have concerns that need to be addressed as well.

❂ Observe his response: Notice not only the words he uses but also the words he avoids. Pay attention to his body language. Is he crossing his arms in a defensive posture? Or is he leaning into you, looking into your eyes, and stroking your hand in a caring and loving way? If he demonstrates anger by overreacting to your talk, you're in an abusive relationship. (Don't stick around in case his anger escalates.) If he tells you that he thinks of you as a 'friend,' consider this code for, *I don't want to hurt your feelings by saying I don't love you or that you're not my type.*

❂ Choose to compromise: Rarely is one or the other 100% right or wrong. In all relationships there are compromises. For instance if you tell him that you want to step up the relationship and he admits he feels a strong attachment to you but that he needs more time, come up with some choices: 1. Set a timeline for him to figure it out and then talk again. 2. Suggest couples counseling. 3. Let him know you aren't sitting on a shelf waiting. Make no false threats and mean what you say. It's not about ultimatums; it's about choices.

❂ Convey your needs: If you tell him you aren't feeling secure about his love for you and he responds, *"I care [love, cherish, or other such terms] for you. Tell me what else I must do to prove this to you."* Tell him what you need. He might assume you understand he loves you when he does things (rewires your electronics, helps in the yard, fixes your flat tire, invites you to his parents' anniversary dinner, takes you to the lake for the weekend, etc.). You, on the other hand, might need to be told *I-love-you* with an engagement ring on your finger. If communication between the two of you is missing the mark, share what your needs are and ask him what his are. You two might only need to tweak the heart vibe to resonate *I love you* more clearly.

○ <u>End on a high note</u>: Wrap it up in a courteous note, regardless of whether or not it went the way you hoped. If you feel the relationship is on track, great. But if you feel it best to part ways, then saying goodbye in a kind and civil way keeps the heart whole and your dignity intact.

○ <u>No quick fixes</u>: Let's say *The Talk* was a step in the right direction and things are improving. Males need to be reassured they are respected. So praise his efforts on what he's doing right but resist the urge to nag when things go off track. Anticipate set-backs that may need another round of talks. Seek progress without aiming for perfection.

Key Points
Rules 4 Having *The Talk*

♻ **<u>Wait until your emotions are calm.</u>** Otherwise, tempers may flair, escalating the talk into a yelling match. To regain composure, journal through your emotions until you can cut through the diatribe in a concise and simple way with no more than three talking points. Rehearse what you wish to say and then set up a meeting. Tell him how much time you need and ask him, *When is a good time to talk?*

♻ **<u>Use "I" statements.</u>** Speak from your heart by sharing how you feel about the problem and tell him what you desire. Avoid blaming and shaming. Your goal is to open up communication, not shut it down.

♻ **<u>Pause and listen.</u>** Don't nag. After stating your concerns, allow him a chance to share his thoughts. Listen and observe *how* he responds. Notice his body language.

♻ **<u>Look for resolution and understanding.</u>** Healthy relationships are never a one-way street. They are supported by compromises. The hope is that the two of you will come to a mutual agreement. There may be a training period — a few adjustments along the way needing a follow-up talk. Don't forget to praise his efforts!

YOU FEEL SAFE TO BE
YOURSELF AND TALK
ABOUT ANYTHING
TOGETHER.

Loving Relationship

Questions 'n Reflections (QnR)
Preparing for *The Talk*

Healthy relationships are built upon trust, but trust requires honest communication. When he's sending mixed messages or none at all and your gut senses something is amiss, it's up to you to initiate an understanding before the relationship completely falls apart. To prepare for *The Talk*, ask yourself:

What are my "I" statements? What is it I need from him to feel secure in this relationship?

What is the best outcome of this talk, and how do I hope to get there together?

What important talking points must I emphasize to stay on message?

How will I end the talk if it becomes argumentative?

What compromises am I prepared and willing to make for this relationship to continue?

If after having a talk I discover the relationship is not working, how do I articulate that it is over without pointing to blame and shame? In other words, how do you bow out gracefully?

Step 12: Quit Craving Unrequited Love
Start Loving

Sergeant Bill, a goat from Saskatchewan, gained glory and fame as the lucky charm of the Fifth Canadian Battalion in France during World War I. Legend has it he knocked three soldiers into a trench saving their lives seconds before a shell burst precisely where they were standing. He himself was gassed and wounded in battle. In spite of it all, he enjoyed sharing canteen beer with his fellow soldiers and proudly marched in the Victory Europe parade emblazoned with sergeant stripes on his blue plush coat. ~ Source: *The Backyard Goat* by Sue Weaver.

In the battlefields, Sergeant Bill knew firsthand (or hoof) what it takes to live life to its fullest. For those of us in the dating fields, it's do or die trying. Be brave, goatgal! A love quest is not about chasing after whimsical fantasies or pining over a lost love. It's not about play-dating like adolescents. It's about not flinching or bolting when it's genuine. Real love requires us to soldier up and grow up in a wholehearted way.

We all know this, but in spite of it all, we (at least most of us) at some time in our lives pin our heart to another's unloving heart, obsessing someday that they will be ours. Deep down we know they never will. All the while, the good ones slip away.

So, why would a wholehearted goatgal waste time craving love when there are available wholehearted bucks in the field? Could it be because true love requires us to be vulnerable and, fearing heartbreak, we shun from real life dating experiences?

Leon F. Seltzer, Ph.D., in the *Psychology Today* article " Evolution of the Self," explains, "An 'untried' love is virtually without limits precisely because, never really having begun, there's been no time for disillusionment to set in. The beloved — frequently distant, uninterested, unavailable, or unapproachable — can remain an object of indefinite idealization."

Feeling vulnerable is the first step to feeling in love.

Getting past the fantasy of a perfect love and into one that is real requires us to expose tender emotions, imperfections and self doubts — vulnerability. When we do, a wholehearted connection can occur.

Yet those skittish from past unhealed heartaches often disengage at the first sign of conflict. Scared to delve deeper, some of us look for reasons to shut down and bolt at the slightest annoyance, such as his habit of clipping his nails while watching too much basketball.

To stay the course once the newness of the relationship wears off and realness sets in, take a deep breath and assess the meaning of mature love. It's much more than a euphoric high skipping through the tulips. Beyond the schoolgirl giddiness of its first blush, love teaches us much: tolerance, humility, patience, caring, understanding, etc. All those ingredients one needs to endure the challenges of life together. The Beatles sang it simply: "*All you need is love.*" Yes, all you need is real mature love…to share.

Cheryl met her future husband standing in line to vote. Her gift of gab and friendly personality captured Jim's attention. The attraction was evident and they began dating. After three months of casual dating, they stepped the relationship up to "exclusive," proclaiming their love for one another.

Some months later, Jim's love grew stronger. He desired more time with Cheryl and suggested they move in together.

Cheryl, who grew up in a strict religious home, told Jim that even though she loved him she wanted the promise of marriage before living together. Jim, who was currently employed plus aiming toward a Master's degree, had intended to marry Cheryl once his career goals were reached. After some negotiating, they agreed to officially announce their engagement to their family and friends with a wedding date chosen for a year later.

They shared their love but could they share a closet?

Cheryl moved into her fiancé's humble one-bedroom, one-bathroom apartment. Soon after, she grew dismayed at the small closet and having to take turns sharing a bathroom. She became edgy and short-tempered while silently stewing over her decision to trade her apartment for such cramped quarters.

The realness of living together created stress on their loving relationship. Feeling vulnerable and not knowing which direction to take, she chose to talk it over by confessing her doubts. She used "I" statements as discussed in the previous *Talk Tips*, asserting her love for him but explaining that the accommodations were less than what she was accustomed to. Jim was relieved she had opened up instead of running away in silence. He reassured her that the small apartment was only temporary. Their talk alleviated Jim's worries over Cheryl's moodiness. The tension in the air was cleared and Cheryl felt a closer connection to Jim and vice versa.

That was twenty-one years ago. More recently, they celebrated their twentieth wedding anniversary surrounded by their kids. Jim toasted his wife: "To my best friend, lover, and mother of my kids, I knew we would make it when you sacrificed half your wardrobe to fit in our one closet."

"Love is not something we give or get; it is something that we nurture and grow, a connection that can only be cultivated between two people when it exists within each one of them – we can only love others as much as we love ourselves." ~ Brené Brown

Key Points
Rules 4 Loving

- **Quit craving unrequited love**. Assess whether or not you are more often fixated on an unobtainable *perfect* love and bolt when things start to feel real. If so, look inward to unravel why (Steps 1-3).

- **Get Real!** Once the blush of romance fades and realness sets in, assess the meaning of mature love. Embrace its lessons: tolerance, humility, patience, caring, understanding, etc. This becomes the glue that holds your relationship together.

- **Allow vulnerability.** Love is not perfect, and neither are you. When you hit bumps in the road, examine those issues and seek resolution just as you have in repairing your heart. The more effort you invest, the more value, love and care you place in the relationship.

- **Release control.** Once trust and love are set, lean into his arms effortlessly. And when things come up (as happens in all relationships), do you part in seeking understanding.

BEING VULNERABLE
TOGETHER DOESN'T
FEEL RISKY.

Loving Relationship

Questions 'n Reflections (QnR)
Stop Craving and Start Loving

Since childhood, Hollywood captivated us with *happily ever after* and idyllic versions of romances. In adulthood, some of us still cling to the notion that love is elusive, save only for a select few on the silver screen. Truth is, it's available to anyone willing to be open-hearted and realistic. Ask yourself this:

What are the tell-tale signs that a relationship is one-sided? Are you typically drawn to a certain unattainable type? If so, why?

Am I craving a long lost relationship, secretly hoping he will return (or other love obsession that isn't real)? If so, what's it going to take for you to wake up from that dream?

Am I carrying a torch because I believe no one else will match up? If so, are you clamping down your heart by setting unattainable expectations as an excuse not to love? Explain why.

Do I have improbable expectations because I enjoy the fantasy of euphoric romance more than mature love? If so, explain what the payoff is.

What do I typically do when a relationship starts to feel real? If you are skittish and more often guilty of ending it on the first off-key note, explain why.

In the future, what am I willing to do in remaining open-hearted once the excitement of a new relationship wears off? An honest look within softens the shortcomings in others.

.

Step 13: Breakup Etiquette
Make Room for Love

In the movie *Men Who Stare at Goats*, Jeff Bridges plays the role of Bill Django, who claims to be able to stop the heart of a goat by merely staring at it, a tactic used in a psychic military exercise.

Getting into a relationship is easy. You're filled with the hope and exhilaration that he's the one, then—Oops!—your heart freezes and you're stared-down with the realization that he's not the one. Truth be told, an evening home alone trimming your hooves is a more tempting option than a night on the town with him. Now what? Do you quietly fade away, not answer his calls and texts, hoping he, too, will go away? That tactic might work if it's been a casual relationship, but if it's a more serious or exclusive one there must be an official (and hopefully a dignified) goodbye.

Making the decision to get out is never easy, especially if emotions are heavily invested. There could be levels of guilt, indicating that you aren't being honest with yourself. (If so, you may want to consult a therapist or attend couple's counseling.) So, you drag it out, second-guessing your decision and hoping for the right moment, but there is no "right moment."

Meanwhile, time marches on and you put it off because you don't want to hurt him. But hiding behind your true feelings is dishonest, deceptive and, ultimately, hurtful to you and him. Pretending you care for someone when you don't is cheating both of you out of a chance at true love (with someone else).

Anna was in an unhappy long-term relationship (three years) with Phil. The relationship got off to a rocky start from day one. There were suspicions and jealousies from both of them, but the make-up sex held them together. Other than their sexual chemistry, they had nothing in common. He was laid-back with a *devil-may-care* attitude. She was ambitious and hard-working. In some relationships, these attributes can meld and compliment one another. In their case, resentments built with underlying trust issues. Anna held on to the relationship because she felt she owed it to Phil for stealing him away from his previous relationship. By their third year together, she caught him cheating on her. Relieved, she had reason to cut and run and make him her scapegoat.

When you know it's not right, you needn't look for a reason beyond the truth…that you had a change of heart. As awkward as it is to utter *it's over* to someone whom you once told *I love you*, you must. As you do, honor what you two shared by speaking from your heart without adding shame and blame. A cordial goodbye, preferably face to face, allows official closure for the both of you. Once you've left, you can then begin the task of cleaning up the emotional fallout and clearing the way for the right one.

Warning! For those in an abusive relationship (physical, mental, and/or emotional), breaking up can be a dangerous trigger. Abusers thrive on control. When things shift out of their control, they retaliate in a raging panic and, too often, with violence aimed at you, family members, pets, personal property, or towards themselves (threatening suicide). Have a cautious exit strategy *before* you break up. Consult the police or contact a women's shelter. For more advice, visit a domestic violence website such as the www.ncadv.org.

"A relationship, I think, is like a shark. You know? It has to constantly move forward or it dies. And I think what we got on our hands is a dead shark." ~ Alvy Singer (Woody Allen) in *Annie Hall*

Breakup Tips

The following breakup tips apply *only* to those leaving a non-abusive relationship.

☙ Just do it! There's never a good time to break up or the perfect reason to call it off. Even so, your heart knows when a relationship is right and when it's wrong. When the decision is clear, tell him you need to talk. You set the time/place.

☙ Meet on neutral turf. A restaurant, coffee shop or other public locale and in separate cars is best. You hope it's an amicable goodbye, but if it turns out otherwise, have your say and then leave. If you can't meet in person, then a phone call will do. Texting or emailing is undignified and you may not know whether he received your message. If he senses you are going to break up and he avoids meeting with you, then you have no choice but to call and leave a message.

☙ Be courteous. Speak straightforwardly while using "I" statements as outlined in *Talk Tips*. No blaming and/or shaming (no scapegoating). This way you aren't building a case against him, which would only launch into an argument. Be kind but clear and to the point. If that doesn't work, don't argue back and forth. End the discussion by telling him *goodbye* and then leave.

☙ Expect a reaction. If he becomes emotional (but not raging), find peaceful closure by talking through the tender moments shared. If he becomes angry or manipulative by saying you can't leave him or that he can't live without you, don't drag the inevitable out any longer. Tell him *goodbye* and then go.

✪ Can we be friends? If he asks, tell him, *Sure* (assuming you are on reasonably good terms), but be clear that you think it's best to leave each other alone for now, until the emotions subside. More often, *friendship* is used as a ploy to maintain the relationship, which only delays the official breakup.

✪ Denial. He may initially have been blindsided and, therefore, ask for another meeting with you to help him process through the breakup. If so, stay on message as you did before. But if this becomes a plea for attention and he continues to insist on seeing you, don't give in. He will soon get the message and move on. If he doesn't leave you alone — he's stalking and harassing--contact the police for assistance.

✪ No gossiping. It's undignified to publicly rehash the sordid details of a relationship you once shared privately. It serves no purpose except to stir up the pot. If others pry, shrug your shoulders and say, *It just didn't work out.*

Key Points
Rules 4 Breaking Up*

○ **Meet face-to-face.** It's preferable to give dignity to the relationship you once shared by meeting in person (unless there's been abuse) rather than breaking up over the phone or texting. Meet on neutral turf. This way, you can say your goodbyes and leave sooner if things don't go smoothly.

○ **Be clear.** Use the "I" statements. (Example: *I feel there is no need to continue this relationship because my feelings have changed.*) Refrain from shaming or blaming, which could ignite a dramatic argument.

○ **Be kind and compassionate.** There's nothing pleasant or easy about breaking up. To make it less hurtful, talk through the tender moments shared to honor what you did have. This helps with closure and allows space for healing the heart.

○ **No gossiping.** Being in a relationship is a private matter, and so is exiting one. To avoid the fallout of a breakup, avoid gossiping to his or your friends, which will only stir the pot and prolong the aftermath. Instead, simply state, *"It just didn't work out."* In time, your breakup will be old news.

*These apply to a non-abusive relationship only.

HE WAS YOUR
REBOUND AFTER A
BAAAD BREAKUP.
YOU DID IT HOPING TO
FORGET THE PAIN.
IT ONLY MADE IT
WORSE.

Roll in the Hay

Questions 'n Reflections (QnR)
Breakup Readiness

When breaking up is done recklessly, there's a risk of jumping into another relationship too soon as a rebound from the last. As you ponder through the agonizing decision in getting out of a relationship, ask yourself:

Was he wrong for me or was I wrong for him? Not all relationships are clearly right or wrong. Looking back, were there early signs this wasn't a good match? If so, explain what those warning signs were and why you overlooked them.

Am I struggling over whether or not to break up because I feel guilty and, thus, second guessing my decision? If so, in what way have you not been honest with yourself? Explain how and why you have sacrificed your needs for another. It could be that you withheld a part of yourself.

Am I leaving this relationship because something unexpected happened or was it just a change of heart? When two people form a relationship, it often takes on a life of its own. For awhile it could flow in perfect harmony until a monkey wrench gets thrown in the mix. When that happens, the dynamics change either for good or for bad. If so, explain the wrench.

What have I learned from this relationship that better prepares me for the next? Each heartfelt relationship offers deeper insight into love. When it ends, we choose to either shut down our hearts or remain open-hearted, depending on lessons learned and memories shared. What wisdom and memories did you take from this?

Step 14: OMG...I've Been Dumped!

Long ago, a goat fell off a passing truck and wandered into Chicago's Lincoln Tavern. Its owner, William Sianis (who later became known as *Billy Goat* Sianis), adopted the *fallen* goat as his pet, grew a goatee and changed the name of the tavern to the Billy Goat Tavern. On October 6th 1945, *Billy Goat* took his pet goat Murphy to see the Cubs play at the World Series. Upon getting kicked out of the game because Murphy stunk, *Billy Goat* declared a curse on the Cubs. The rest is history.

Getting dumped is awful and it does stink, but it's part of the uncertainty of dating. One day you feel like you fell off a truck, and the next, your luck changes and true love wanders in. For now, your blood pressure has spiked and your mind is racing. You thought he loved you—maybe he did—and then he didn't. Or he found someone else, lost interest or simply wanted out. A goat rarely will utter *I don't love you anymore*. Most will do and say anything else but admit the cold-hearted truth for fear you will cry, pitch a fit or slice off his...*ahem*... family jewels. He may tell you he needs time to sort things out or that he wants to be *friends*. Maybe he just went away and stopped calling without any explanation. It doesn't matter how or what he told you, you got the message—you've been dumped!

Your friends tell you he was a low-life and that you deserve better. They want to cheer you up and fix you up with so-and-so who is really nice, but such words fall flat because your heart aches. Well, more than aches...it's hemorrhaging! The thought of going out on a date is not on your to-do list. You'd rather stick a dagger in your heart; it wouldn't hurt as bad. You lament, *"I give up! I can't bear the thought of giving my heart away EVER again."*

You're right to feel hurt, depressed, dismayed and angry. You may even look to find fault with him or, worse, with yourself. While processing the discomfort of your loss, watch the types of words you use and be mindful of catastrophic expressions that undermine your worth: *How could he hurt me this way? What kind of a creep could do this to me? After all I did for him! If only I were sexier, prettier, smarter or skinnier.* Instead, tell the tale that empowers you instead of shames you: *It was fun while it lasted. It's not the end of my world. The next one just might be the right one!*

As you know from working through all the previous QnR's, your broken heart will heal once you discover the wisdom, let go of the pain and move forward. For now, the shock of your loss is reeling and the only release from torment is an hour's workout topped off with a pint of Ben & Jerry's *"Chocolate Therapy."*

Beware of vengeful behavior!

After dusting yourself off from getting tossed to the curb, don't let him *get your goat.* At first, you might take it on the chin, but later strange thoughts of revenge seep in, triggered by a song or the news that he's with someone else. When your blood boils, take a breather. Don't act out and regret it later. In *Fatal Attraction*, Glenn Close's character sought revenge on Michael Douglas' character by stewing the family's pet rabbit; but it didn't end there. In the final scene, her vengeance destroyed her.

They say the best revenge is living a good and joyful life. Keep that in mind as you transform a dreary ending into a bright new beginning. You'll know you're relationship ready when you stop obsessing over what went wrong and come to realize you two just weren't right for each other. One day, you'll look back with gratitude that he did you a favor by going away. Until then, do what it takes to work through the bitter emotions by surrounding yourself with trusted friends and family and other such ways to nurture self, heart and ego (Step 4). If need be, work through the harsh lessons learned by reviewing Steps 1-3.

The last time I got dumped, it took me by surprise. Looking back, though, there was a warning sign. He told me on the first date that he wasn't interested in a serious relationship. I didn't believe him. I suspect, as time passed and the newness wore off, it started to feel more serious to him so he bolted before he got in too deep. Nevertheless, when it happened I felt like discarded goods. I couldn't help but think there was something about me that didn't measure up. Then the anger set in and I wondered if he found someone else. It took me awhile to learn this lesson: *He never was interested in a relationship. Therefore, it wasn't about me after all.* Once I figured that out, the anger lifted, my self-esteem recovered, and I knew I was ready to venture back into those dating fields…a bit wiser, too.

It's over when you can go on a date and not talk about your ex.

I'm sure you agree, there's nothing more boring than going out on a date with someone who can't stop talking about how *she-done-him-wrong*. It signals, *"Danger! You're their rebound."* Don't risk dating prematurely. Wait it out until your breakup is not on the tip of your tongue. If you need to vent and rehash the details of what happened, do so with a close friend or therapist, not a potential prospect.

"Talk not of wasted affection; affection never was wasted."

~ Henry Wadsworth Longfellow

OMG-I've-Been-Dumped Survival Tips

✿ Feel the pain! Getting dumped is a shock, so expect to feel hurt and sad after the numbness and anger wear off. Go easy on yourself! Your friends might tell you, *He was a jerk*, and it might be the absolute truth, but it is still a loss. You may need to talk it out with a trusted friend or therapist.

✿ It's not personal! Don't beat yourself up. Tell yourself it's not a reflection on your self-worth. Frame the loss in a positive way... two who weren't right for each other, a stepping stone toward true love, a practice run, or other ways that aren't shameful, earth-shattering or degrading.

✿ No begging! When you feel the urge to beg for his love or to look for excuses to see him again, do not! You'll only be setting yourself up for more heartache. If he dumped you once, he'll do it again.

✿ Stop obsessing! No stalking, harassing and gossiping. This will only make you look foolish and, worse yet, you may need to pay an attorney to handle that restraining order. Take some deep breaths and visualize a loving relationship in your near future. If that doesn't work, rent the movie *Fatal Attraction*.

✿ Be in good company. Spend time with those who love you unconditionally.

○ No rebounds! Avoid a hasty romance (roll in the hay) thinking you can bury the pain. It may feel good at the moment, but it's not fair to you or him since you are not relationship ready. Once you have made peace with what happened and you no longer feel the need to talk about it, then you will be ready to date again.

○ Take a break. If you are disheartened and think you want to give up on love, spend time nurturing self to re-gain your confidence and feminine power (as outlined in previous Steps).

○ No acting-out! No binge eating, drinking, drugging, promiscuous sex, or other self-destructive behaviors to numb the hurt. Instead, work off those emotions by join-ing a hiking group, yoga class, etc.

○ Don't weaken! If he contacts you and you sense it is only for a roll in the hay, resist the temptation. He dumped you once; don't let him use and discard you again.

○ Release the emotions. Journal through your emotions and discover your lessons learned, even if it's knowing you will get through this set-back. As you do, your heart will mend, readying itself for love that is here to stay.

Key Points
Rules 4 Getting Dumped

☯ **It's not the end of the world.** Sometimes we're the dump-ee and sometimes we're the dump-er. It happens to the best of us. You'll get over this once your ego and heart are mended. (Review Steps 1-3).

☯ **Sort through the emotions.** Avoid gossip and vengeful behaviors. Instead, journal and talk it out with a trusted friend or therapist to help you move past the emotional trauma.

☯ **Learn its humiliating lesson.** Be mindful of how you articulate this experience by using words that are empowering rather than degrading. *"It was bound to happen sooner or later. I have a feeling the next one will be the right one,"* sets an optimistic tone. Take time to discover its lesson. Once you do, the emotions subside.

☯ **Don't rush into a rebound romance.** Avoid dating too soon, before the emotional debris is released. You're ready to get back out there when you can engage in a conversation without bringing up your ex.

ROLL IN THE HAY

FOR REVENGE AFTER A BREAKUP, YOU DID IT WITH HIS BEST FRIEND. LATER, THEY BOTH SLANDERED YOU ON A SOCIAL NETWORK SITE.

Questions 'n Reflections (QnR)
Wisdom from Getting Dumped

Let's face it, being rejected is painful. If you're not careful, the negativity could morph into prolonged agony by lashing out in destructive ways. To find closure, find the tough lesson learned. As Dr. Phil says, *"Moving past a breakup is about you, not your ex."* Ask yourself:

Did I see it coming or was I blindsided? Upon reflection, there may have been warning signs the relationship didn't have staying power. If so, explain.

How did he end it? Did he tell you his reason? Do you believe him, or do you think it was for some other reason?

How do I feel? Journal through your emotions to release the bitterness out from your heart and onto paper. Getting it out helps to work it out.

How am I responding and/or reacting? If you're angry, do you want revenge? If you're love-sick, are you looking for a way to manipulate him back into your life? Are you considering a rebound to make the pain go away? Be honest! Then ask yourself: *What good would that do?*

If I'm struggling in moving past the breakup, what's my backup plan? Talking it over with a trusted friend or therapist helps to regain your footing. Working the anger off at the gym helps, too.

What did I take from this experience? As dreadful as it is to get dumped, such set-backs are expected when one is on a love quest. Even so, there are gains from losses. What are the lessons learned from this humiliating experience?

Step 15: A Love Connection
How Do You Know?

By nature, goats are herd animals that thrive in the company of others as protection from hungry predators. If you befriend a goat, he'll be happy and content with a constant companion. His owner, another goat, or a small donkey will provide him with the love and attention he needs.

Alone in our empty bed chambers we dream of the day we're safely snuggled up in the arms of a loving mate. Questioning when and if that day will ever come, we set to task repairing our hearts and rehearsing our flirting techniques, memorizing the *Rules 4 Dating* and resolving not to be led astray by a random lustful encounter. Then we put to test *barnyard's wisdom*, cursing its outcome if last weekend's date was more likened to a wildebeest than a genteel suitor; or, the chemistry was there (on your part) but his part fell flat.

So, how do you know he's the one? There are endless volumes of poetry on the subject of love, each one as heartfelt as the other. Suffice it to say, it's a feeling you get when you know your heart is aligned to his. Like a light bulb that warms you up from the inside out, you'll just know. When it happens, it makes all those dating experiences worthwhile, each one leading you there.

"It was a million tiny little things that, when you added them all up, they meant we were supposed to be together...and I knew it."
~ Tom Hanks, *Sleepless In Seattle*

Attributes of a Loving Relationship

These are a few indicators it's heading in the right direction and worth taking a chance at love. (Some you'll recognize from the previous QnR's.)

◊ Doing nothing together is as divine as a night out on the town.

◊ When the going gets tough, you team up in support of one another by saying, *"We're in this together."*

◊ You trust each other, even when you or your partner spends time apart.

◊ You know each other's faults but overlook them while focusing on one another's attributes.

◊ You have much in common, but when there are differences, you both agree to respectfully disagree.

◊ When you make plans together, you consider each other's wishes and are willing to make compromises.

◊ You are supportive of each other's interests, even if such pursuits are separate journeys.

◊ He doesn't pressure you for sex and respects your wishes to hold out until you are ready (and vice versa).

◊ You feel safe to be yourself and talk about anything together.

◊ You understand that another's emotional ups and downs are not always about you.

◊ You can't imagine life without the other. You feel loved, cared for and respected.

- The relationship feels honest, accepting and respectful. It's like being with a close friend...no pretense or pretending.

- Being vulnerable together doesn't feel risky.

- Whether together or when apart, you always feel connected.

- You feel blessed to have each other to share in the joys as well as the sorrows of life.

WHETHER TOGETHER
OR WHEN APART,
YOU ALWAYS FEEL
CONNECTED.

Loving Relationship

Questions 'n Reflections (QnR)
A Love Connection

Love doesn't show up on your doorstep with a neon sign blinking L-O-V-E, but it does tug at your heart. Those happily in love testify, *"I just felt it. I can't describe how I knew he was the one, but I just knew."* To make sense of what a love connection is, tune into your heart's desire. Ask yourself:

How would I describe a loving relationship? Is it caring for another beyond one's own needs? For some it's a dreamy poem with promises of everlasting *I-can't-live-without-you,* and for others it's the foundation for building a family. What's your definition?

Am I ready for a love connection? Is there room for love in your heart *and* your life? If so, explain how you know.

123

Can I be trusted with someone else's heart and vice versa? Opening your heart to *happily-ever-after* and the risk of heartbreak for you and for him tests one's resolve. Explain how *barnyard wisdom* has given you the tools to maneuver the ups and downs of love's quest.

Here's how I know it's a love connection. Listen to your heart's desire. Then imagine you've met and started dating. Now, dive to its depths by scripting a scenario from that first interaction to the moment *you just knew*.

Afterword

It's been two years since I embarked on the *GoatGal's Dating MANual*. I've taken you with me, dear reader, in healing the heart and then testing it again.

I must lay bare my confessions. While weaving through these Steps, I've had romantic encounters (good and *baahd*). Some, I admit, I barged into recklessly and stumbled out of ungracefully. Others were less goatish and began with hopeful promise but fizzled into a lackluster friendship. Then *love* showed up. It wasn't a rising crescendo over a moonlit night or a platinum diamond ring placed on my finger. It was a deeply felt connection impossible to describe.

I stalled and postponed writing this final Step as I carried on with my routines, friendships, and in-the-trenches dating experiences. I've learned there's no way to fast forward through the drama of dating to get to the best part—*happily ever after*. If we could, we would skip all those ecstatic highs and crashing lows and everything betwixt and between. But without those emotional tests, you wouldn't know how resilient your heart is and what it desires. And that it's not so much about the search for another's heart of gold as it is more about connecting to one's own. And it takes those interpersonal encounters to bring out the worst and the best, to feel the pain when it's wrong and to feel the joy when it's right.

Throughout love's quest, remain steadfast. It's not *only* about what's out there waiting; love waits patiently for *you* to show up. The rest is easy…for you *are* love, my beloved!

About the Author

Peggy Kligman resides in El Paso, TX. She and her family settled there when she was nine. Once grown, she moved away to explore life and returned later to rear a family of her own and to enjoy the goat farms nearby. An entrepreneur, motivational speaker, game inventor and facilitator of Goat Game events, she advocates for healthy relationships and dating behaviors while speaking out against domestic violence. She is happily *single* while blessed with the love of family and friends and a special someone.